African American Entrepreneurs

African American Entrepreneurs

Successes and Struggles of Entrepreneurs of Color in America

Michelle Ingram Spain and J. Mark Munoz

 BUSINESS EXPERT PRESS

African American Entrepreneurs: Successes and Struggles of Entrepreneurs of Color in America

First published in 2018 by
Business Expert Press, LLC
222 East 46th Street, New York, NY 10017
www.businessexpertpress.com

ISBN-13: 978-1-60649-358-8 (paperback)
ISBN-13: 978-1-60649-359-5 (e-book)

Business Expert Press Entrepreneurship and Small Business Management Collection

Collection ISSN: 1946-5653 (print)
Collection ISSN: 1946-5661 (electronic)

Cover and interior design by Exeter Premedia Services Private Ltd., Chennai, India

First edition: 2018

10 9 8 7 6 5 4 3 2 1

Printed in the United States of America.

Abstract

African American entrepreneurs are key contributors to the American economy. Faced with numerous challenges, many African American entrepreneurs have learned to transcend tough obstacles, leverage resources, and strategically pursue opportunities to achieve business success. This book captures the stories and mindsets of contemporary African Americans in their quest for the American dream.

Keywords

African American entrepreneurship, entrepreneurship, minority entrepreneurship

Contents

Preface

According to Webster's dictionary, an entrepreneur is a person who "organizes, manages, and assumes the risks of a business enterprise." In 1986, Peter Drucker defined entrepreneurship as the process of gathering and allocating the financial, creative, managerial, or technological resources necessary for a new venture's success. Bygrave (1997) went further, stating that it is the essence of any free enterprise for the birth of a new business to give a market economy its vitality. Brodsky (1996) expanded the definition to: "Starting with nothing more than an idea or a prototype, entrepreneurs can take a business to the point at which it can sustain itself on an internally generated cash flow." According to Murphy (2014), a columnist for Inc. Magazine, Harvard University teaches a 12-word definition of an entrepreneur, "Entrepreneurship is the pursuit of opportunity without regard to resources currently controlled." Additionally, positive mindset is crucial since it can impact venture viability (Huang and Pearce 2015). The network of threads constructed to support an idea, organize, manage, a calculated risk by the African American entrepreneur when compared is similar. Some instinctively learned from the calculated risk they assumed when starting a business others did not. Some developed the skill necessary to succeed; others did not. The authors define the entrepreneur as the individual with an innate survival instinct willing to learn, adapt, and apply the skills they learn through observation and reflection, not the classroom.

The entrepreneurs' ancestors, upon whom this book focuses, entered America as unwilling immigrants. There is a full breadth of cultural practices, beliefs, and value systems that dominate African American entrepreneurship in America that began during slavery. They developed an ability to assume calculated risk, apply "just -in time" strategies and knowledge to gather and distribute resources during slavery. During slavery and post-slavery, their entrepreneurial experiences are unique. They did not control resources, yet, they pursued opportunities. They generated economic vitality in the African American community and made enough cash flow to their businesses to make a difference in the quality of their lifestyle and the economic sustainability of the African American community.

The range of facts and assumptions about African Americans often send situational cues to African American entrepreneurs signaling awareness, knowledge, and problem-solving strategies. One way of trying to embrace the various facts and assumptions that drive the African American businessmen's experience is to write about the owners' shared experiences and viewpoints. This includes the links to their backgrounds, social histories, success or failure, as well as the pursuit of opportunities with scarce resources.

In a perfectly uniformed entrepreneurial world, all entrepreneurs would not be alike. Race, gender, ethnicity, social learning history, emotional intelligence, social capital transactions, access to opportunities and resources would cause imbalance. It is easy for many to attribute race as the primary throttle that divides entrepreneurial uniformity. The race-based public laws, executive orders, regulations, and requirements often increase or decrease the opportunities for African American entrepreneurs.

In this book, the authors explore the experiences of the African American business owner, who is the principal in various small business initiatives, industries, and geographic locations. They link his/her business to the race-based throttle controlled by state and local public laws, executive orders, regulations, and requirements for doing business as an African American business owner regardless of gender. This throttle controls the playing fields, and the designated business zones in which African American entrepreneurs do business. If the business owner elects to take advantage of self-employment opportunities, supportive services, and resources, such as access to capital, insurance and bonding, business support services, projects and procurement opportunity options controlled by mainstream America, they conduct their business in the designated zone.

In the book, African American entrepreneurs discuss how entrepreneurship, for them, is a transected process driven by assumptions about their race.

There are several reasons why the authors wrote this book. Entrepreneurship, as a topic embraced by the American educational system, is the newest subject in the academic curriculum in universities as well as grades K thru 12. According to Carl J. Schramm (Entrepreneurship in Higher Education 2017), Kauffman Foundation President and CEO: "Like philosophy or music, entrepreneurship is a field of study that generates—rather than discovers or encounters its subject matter. Unlike history, sociology, or anthropology, for instance, entrepreneurship creates what it studies."

Entrepreneurship in the urban and rural communities accelerates economic change and sustainability. As a result, state and local governments, nonprofit economic development organizations and foundations, and higher education institutions are focusing on venture development and innovation as an economic sustainability and community transformation tool in urban and rural communities. Public Laws and executive orders are executed to ensure African American and other ethnic minority business owners receive equal access to assistance and support services and opportunities for their businesses. Political, social, economic development transformations in mainstream America forced African American entrepreneurs to develop their own strategies, for the inclusion of minority and women-owned businesses in local and national levels. These entrepreneurs sought economic betterment and pursued new venture opportunities typically in the small and medium sized business categories.

The entrepreneurs taking part in the interviews came from all walks of life. Some were seasoned business persons, others were young entrepreneurs, and still, others were serial entrepreneurs starting businesses to "make due," support their families and sustain their lifestyle. Some were highly educated, others were not, and some were ex-offenders, veterans, single parents, and disabled. The responses represent a diverse group of entrepreneurs, viewpoints, and profiles.

Oral storytelling, social learning histories, and the motivation to build a business unlock the desire to succeed as an entrepreneur. The post-survey interviews, exploration of commonality in business venture stories being told by family and community elders, reflective thinking approaches to entrepreneurship and their lifestyles are included. The authors did not bundle together or generalize African American attitudes. They explored African American entrepreneurs' strategies, day-to-day business operations, and access to opportunities. During the interviews, it soon became apparent that responses to each question tended to be different. Each entrepreneur processed issues and exchanges with the authors during the one-on-one discussions differently. The entrepreneurs distinctively articulated their thoughts. Answers came from various directions often driven by situational experiences that resulted in the entrepreneurs emerging on diverse entrepreneurial paths. Each interview was unique and seemed motivated by the entrepreneurs' social learning, social capital histories, and their interpretation of situational cues throttled by their race. The survey offered insight into:

- What makes the African American entrepreneur tick?
- Why are African American entrepreneurs "different from mainstream American entrepreneurs and other ethnic minorities?"
- What were the motivators for African American entrepreneurs' success?
- What challenges did African American entrepreneurs face?
- How were these challenges overcome?
- Why is the African American entrepreneurs' story unique?

The entrepreneurs' social learning histories made uncovering their reasons for becoming entrepreneurs challenging. They also spoke volumes concerning the high level of self-hood ("I" and "Me"), the person in the mirror, their social contract, responsibility, and self-reward controls requirements as these people pursuing the American dream of becoming successful entrepreneurs. They were their own story.

African American business owners self-regulate. They resonate similar social learning, social capital, emotional intelligence, and survival instincts. Storytelling traditions prompt reflective dialogues. Storytelling illuminates the bonds to ancestors, American descendants of Africans who were unwilling immigrants to America. These dialogues include insights on their cultural expectations, time perspective, reward reinforcement, and self-imposed demands for perfection in their business and community linked to race and self-reflection. Additionally, their interpretation and reaction to race-based situational cues are explored.

The book structure is simple: Acknowledgment and a Preface; Chapter 1 Introduction; Chapter 2 Research Overview and Context; Chapter 3 the African American Entrepreneur Interviews; Chapter 4 Analysis of the Findings ; and Chapter 5 Conclusion and Discussion.

The authors hope that readers will find the stories and insights behind the contemporary African American entrepreneurs enlightening and inspiring.

References

Brodsky, N. 1996. "The Three Criteria for Successful New Business." *Inc (April 1996) in Annual Editions Entrepreneurship* 99, p. 48.

Bygrave, W.D. 1997. "The Entrepreneurial Process." In *The Portable MBA in Entrepreneurship,* ed. W.D. Bygrave. New York, NY: John Wiley Sons.

Drucker, P. 1986. *The Executive in Action.* New York, NY: Harper Collins.

Entrepreneurship in Higher Education. 2017. *Entrepreneurship in Higher Education,* available at http://docplayer.net/5662783-Entrepreneurship-in-American-higher-education.html (accessed July 27, 2017).

Huang, L., and J.L. Pearce. 2015. "Managing the Unknowable: The Effectiveness of Early-Stage Investor Gut Feel in Entrepreneurial Investment Decisions." *Administrative Science Quarterly* 60, pp. 634–70.

Murphy, B. 2014. *50 Ways to Find Co-Founders,* available at https://inc.com/bill-murphy-jr/50-ways-to-find-co-founders.html (accessed July 30, 2017).

CHAPTER 1

Introduction

When we finally achieve the full right of participation in American life, what we make of it will depend upon our sense of cultural values, and our creative use of freedom, not upon our racial identification. I see no reason the heritage of world culture—which represents a continuum—should be confused with the notion of race.

—Ralph Ellison

In 2017, when mainstream Americans start or expand a business, they explore the information and resources made available to all business owners, attend business development workshops, information sessions, and register with small business assistance programs in their local community. This book explores the inconsistency between access to opportunities and information by African American entrepreneurs and non-African American entrepreneurs in the United States of America.

When an entrepreneur opts to classify their business as 51 percent minority-owned and operated, the entrepreneur has also decided to adhere to the local, state, and national legislation, and regulations for minority-owned and operated businesses. The rules of engagement harness the inclusion of the minority business owner. Inclusion, however, is not always fair. Business owners choosing to operate their business as minority-owned are assigned a designated set-aside playing field for minority business, simultaneously conducting business on mainstream America's playing field and comply with dual rules of engagement. The guidelines and adherence to specific rules of engagement for two separate and distinct playing fields are demanding. The playing fields specify what, where, when, how, and with whom a minority business owner can pursue opportunities.

The duality of the rules of engagement requires active learning, emotional intelligence, just in time strategies and calculated risk-taking.

Moreover, businesses classified as minority-owned and operated endure mainstream America's race-based assumptions that the classification providing equal access to business opportunities is at a premium.

The strict federal state and local laws and regulations define the percentage set aside for minority business owners' options for engagement, based on their legally defined status as a minority business. This process results in African American and other minority entrepreneurs of color experiencing the "boomerang" effect.

The boomerang for African American entrepreneurs in 2017 underscores the significance of being descendants of slaves, the unwilling immigrants to the United States of America. The boomerang incisively affected what their ancestors experienced during slavery and the post-civil war era. The slaves were assigned a designated task with defined rules and regulations on the plantations, based on the slave owners or slave merchant's assumptions about the slave's capability, the potential for service or product delivery, based on their external characteristics and gender.

March 5, 1969, the Office of Minority Business Enterprise (Minority Business Development Agency (MBDA) within the United States of America Department of Commerce) was established by President Richard M. Nixon to promote business opportunities for minorities. President Nixon recognized the importance of minority businesses on the nation's economy. In 1983, President Reagan signed Executive Order 11458,34, FR 4937,169, WL9645(Pres) to overcome race-based inequities. He directed federal agencies to develop goals and plans for minority businesses to sell their services and products to the federal, state, local government. Presidents Nixon and Reagan laws generated a boomerang designed to move back and forth between African American and mainstream American entrepreneurs. African American entrepreneurs because of their social learning history, at once understood the importance and the consequences of the federal legislation regarding local engagement.

The participants in the survey emphasized the dichotomy "duality" of their business and lifestyle. As their businesses developed, the business and the entrepreneur changed. These changes occurred in both their social and business environments. Social history provided the owners with a business and lifestyle frame for duality. Most of the owners grew up with a strong social history throttled by care, values, faith, and the desire to self-reward through achieving their goals and dreams. As entrepreneurs, they developed an understanding of the linkages between the chain of events binding the inequities to their social status, race, and ethnicity, the regulations, and requirements throttling the minority business owners' access to opportunities with and through mainstream America.

The uneasiness of these mixed situational cues places pressure on African American entrepreneurs within their own social and race-based groups. These owners are from similar backgrounds, locale, or cultural origin. They often interconnect interest, traditions, and mutual business and family ties. They share bonds that may work to their advantage and disadvantage, often resulting in a mosaic of groups within a group. The interconnection necessitates duality in roles and behaviors resulting in the entrepreneur experiencing a boomerang effect.

In the book, *Invisible Man*, Ellison (1952, p. 3) captures this mindset in this statement:

> *All my life I had been looking for something, and everywhere I turned someone tried to tell me what it was. I accepted their answers too, though they were often in contradiction and even self-contradictory. I was naive. I was looking for myself and asking everyone except myself questions which I, and only I, could answer. It took me a long time and much painful boomeranging of my expectations to achieve a realization everyone else appears to have been born with: that I am nobody but myself.*

In this study and book project, the authors wanted to understand the positivism of African American entrepreneur. Specifically, answers to the questions: If African American entrepreneurs pursue the American dream as a race-based business, does it positively affect the business? If not, why not? What is the impact of race-based programs on their pursuit of the American dream?

African Americans have understood the implications of discrimination and access to the necessary resources for business ventures for centuries. They have also recognized that as entrepreneurs, regardless of race, ethnicity, or gender, they share the same motivation and desire to achieve the American dream as the owner of any profitable and sustainable business.

The authors explored the interconnection between the elements and parts of the laws and legislation, which appear to push African American entrepreneurs forward and pull them backward linking them to mainstream American history. The African American entrepreneurs' stories are the starting point for this exploration.

In 2017, when an entrepreneur starts or expands a small business, there is significant preparation. They explore the information and resources available on the Internet, attend microenterprise information sessions, and enroll in small business workshops, or virtual or classroom small business courses. The entrepreneur also generally finds a qualified small business consultant or registers with a small business assistance program in their local community or a program committed to servicing entrepreneurs. When the entrepreneur exploring the opportunities for launching or expanding small businesses is of African descent, the government and mainstream America signals the owner to tap into programs designated for the minority entrepreneur and their business. The programs are classified and subcategorized by their gender, race, ethnicity, and business industry. The business person quickly senses that their race and ethnic identity defines the duality works and distinctions in the resources, consultants, business assistance, and projects and procurement opportunities available to them.

When an entrepreneur categorizes the business as minority-owned, launches or expands business in adherence to the government legislation, regulations, and directions to designated business set-aside zones for doing business, they develop their business within the guidelines and specific rules of engagement that are constructed carefully defining who they are as minority business owners.

Native American, Asian, Hispanic, and women entrepreneurs experience strict scrutiny as business owners. The result is the aforementioned "boomerang" effect. Specifically, the rules of microenterprise–small business engagement include, but are not limited to the following:

- When, where, and how they do business;
- What opportunities are available;
- How, when, where, and with whom they can develop joint venture projects and collaborations.

This book argues that measures of success, while often subjective, are also seemingly consistent indicators of their probability for achievement. The authors define the entrepreneur as "a person engaged in the process of gathering resources to create and build a microenterprise by leveraging creativity, risk, and innovation." Why? These entrepreneurs link their businesses to a throttle, regardless of their race or gender designated by state and local public laws, executive orders, regulations, requirements, for doing business as business owners. The links, regardless of race or gender, become the throttle that directs and controls their designated business zones. If categorized as an African American entrepreneur, a race-based throttle leads him or her to a designated playing field–business zone in a carefully constructed area set-aside for minority businesses. The playing fields set-aside for businesses owned and operated by minorities become the location of success or failure and business development. The set-aside zone produces threads, creating a web designed to catch business opportunities designated for minorities. The threads used to construct the web, however, are activated by the mainstream American entrepreneur in compliance with the minority set-aside laws, legislation regulations, and rules of engagement.

Mainstream American business owners enjoy unlimited access to supportive services, and resources such as access to capital, insurance, bonding business support services, and access to business options controlled by mainstream America. African American entrepreneurs pursue inclusion and duality that frequently results in an inverted reality.

Most of the interviewees are urban, and they continuously referenced how entrepreneurship, for them, is a process driven by their race and desire for economic independence. Entrepreneurship for this group of men and women is a process without boundaries, which requires the continuous review of their status based on changes in mainstream America and assumptions about their status as qualified business owners, regardless of the race.

Programs designated to provide support services receive funding from the government and other agencies, foundations, and corporations engaged in social responsibility. Political, social, economic, and public transformations and social action in the American culture have forced mainstream America to develop strategies for inclusion of all business owners, regardless of their race and ethnicity. In many communities, local and national, social, and economic development and financial agencies integrate this agenda as part of their economic sustainability strategy.

During the reflective dialogues, the authors discovered that the viewpoints and perceptions of mainstream America's expectations often need duality of mindsets and actions by African American owners. Maintaining roots in the African American community and transitioning into the mainstream American business world is complex and unforgiving. Interviewees also shared how they begin to assume the role of mentors and providers of service, information, and resources in their community, while simultaneously seeking mentors, information, resources, and decision makers in the mainstream American community. Most of the entrepreneurs said that they invest in their communities, purchase property, and others stated that they bought visible portable wealth items such as homes, automobiles, and portable wealth articles to blend in with successful mainstream American entrepreneurs. The owners discussed their inability to develop mainstream American social networks, receive opportunities information promptly, and identify qualified independent business supports resources and databases. The lack of access frequently disrupted the African American male and female entrepreneur's lifestyle, business, and access to the threads required to stabilize their web.

The African American entrepreneur starts with nothing more than a dream. They self-educate or re-educate even if they have formal education, degrees in business, accounting, or law. African American women included in the book share their experiences as not only African American entrepreneurs but also as women entrepreneurs, and how they are expected to assimilate into the "mainstream American woman's" perspective of gender while keeping their "roots" in the African American culture. The authors quickly learned that African American women continue a unique ability to self-regulate based on their description of their social learning history and cultural roots, emotional intelligence, and social capital. The women confirmed their business, personal profiles, and responses to the questionnaires during the follow-up dialogues. They share the impact of the expectations imposed by mainstream America and their African American roots from the kitchen table to the boardroom.

While the answers provided by men and women were not always similar, the questions were standardized. The authors refrain from deviating from the original set of issues except in cases where clarity was essential. The authors also refrained from extracting personal information in respect for their privacy.

The authors spent four years gathering profiles and viewpoints of African American entrepreneurs from diverse backgrounds. Each participant completed the questionnaire. Random in-person interviews, e-mails, and telephone calls validated assumptions raised by the authors. Emphasis placed on the importance of storytelling and social learning histories in their reflections distinguished and differentiated the profiles and viewpoints. For this research, "African American entrepreneurs" refers to men and women who are American citizens of African origin; either born in America or are naturalized citizens and who are engaged in business in America. Some elect to certify their business in the local and national database as minority-owned and operated; others do not. There were no further qualifications. The entrepreneurs interviewed were selected based on success or failure in their industry. Questions concerning their net worth are not part of the profiles. However, net worth was easy to determine from their profile, accomplishments, follow-up discussions, and public information. They have not only survived but also succeeded in America's harsh and challenging business environment.

The gathering of the information for the profiles and viewpoints of African American entrepreneurs offered an opportunity for the authors to gain insights on the entrepreneur and their business approaches. The authors developed a list of 11 questions, specially designed to extract the information they needed, and to encourage the entrepreneurs to discuss their thoughts on the subject openly. The limit to the number of issues is due to sensitivity to the time availability and schedules of these busy entrepreneurs. The impact of this research is a dynamic and thoughtful compilation of insights and viewpoints of African American entrepreneurs in the United States of America. The authors hope that this body of work will serve as an inspiration to existing and new entrepreneurs.

This book tried to offer answers to several business questions. In Table 1.1, the authors list the 11 questions asked and highlight the rationale for each question.

Table 1.1 *Questions rationale*

Kindly offer an overview of your family history. For example, was there an entrepreneur in your family? Did your family history influence your decision to start a business?	To uncover if the family influenced the entrepreneurial decision. Some studies seem to suggest this fact; the authors wanted to confirm if this is the case with African American entrepreneurs.
What was your educational background? Do you have views on formal versus informal education? What are your views on African American entrepreneurial training programs? Has education contributed to your business success?	To understand the role that education played in the entrepreneurial decision and success. The authors also wanted to gain insights whether formal or informal education is preferable.
Starting a new business is not an effortless process. What motivated you to start one? What steps did you take to start the business?	To uncover motivations behind the entrepreneurial start-up.
What challenges did you face when building your business, and how did you overcome them? Did you come across any unique circumstances because of your race?	To explore challenges faced when starting a business enterprise and approaches taken to deal with the problems. The authors wanted to know whether there were racial barriers that African American entrepreneurs needed to overcome.
What types of support were most helpful to you when you were building your business? For example, did your local community play a role in shaping your business interests and development, or was it a mentor? What or who was that one thing that made you believe, "Yes, I can do this!"	To learn about the types of business support most beneficial to African Americans when they build their business. The authors wanted to know whether mentors, organizations, or the local community contributed to business growth.
What skills are essential and required for African American entrepreneurs to succeed in America? Also, what personal attitudes do you think are essential?	To determine what skills and attributes are necessary for African American business success in America. The authors were hoping to identify attitudes and values interwoven into the lifestyles of youth and future entrepreneurs.
If you had the chance to start over again, would you do anything differently? If so, what is the reason?	To gain an understanding of entrepreneurial challenges and mistakes and what can be improved.
How would you characterize the state of African American entrepreneurship in the United States of America? For instance, is it in the first stages, is it growing, or is it mature? Do you think it is open to all or limited to specific individuals? Is it practical from anywhere in the country, or more favorable in individual states?	To gain an understanding of the overall status of African American entrepreneurship in the United States America. The authors wanted to know whether entrepreneurship is for a privileged few or open to everybody. The authors also wanted to gain insights whether individual states present entrepreneurial advantages.

Are you a member of business organizations? Are these groups unique to African Americans or open to all races? Did they contribute to your business success?	To uncover the role business organizations play in the success of African American entrepreneurs.
Do you think social networks and personal connections are essential to business? Did you use networking when building your business, and are your social networks race-based?	To uncover the role social networks and connections play in the success of African American entrepreneurs. The authors also wanted to understand if race played a role in their networking activities.
If you could advise young African American entrepreneurs or other young people thinking about starting a business, what would be the most important consideration and why?	To gain added insights that may be helpful to the African American youth and future entrepreneurs.

The profiles and interviews represent a diverse group of entrepreneurs, viewpoints, and insights.

The authors conducted post-survey interviews to examine commonality in linkages to reflective thinking, storytelling, and social learning histories' approach to entrepreneurship and their lifestyles. The authors did not bundle together or generalize African American entrepreneurial day-to-day operation experiences. However, the insights and viewpoints did explore storytelling and social histories and the entrepreneur's duality, and the boomerang effect of living in a culturally defined world simultaneously with doing business with mainstream America. They explored their strategies, day-to-day business operations, and access to opportunities. During the interviews, it soon became clear that responses to each question tended to be different. The entrepreneurs distinctively articulated their thoughts. Answers came from various directions frequently driven by situational experiences with financial institutions and unions, and designated race-based business playing field, the mandated zone requirements that resulted in the entrepreneurs emerging on diverse entrepreneurial paths.

The road they traveled as business owners made the uncovering of their reasons for becoming entrepreneurs challenging, while it also spoke volumes about the elevated level of self-hood (I and Me), the person in the mirror, and race-based opportunity options. The African American entrepreneur's success and failure were in the range of four vistas:

- Mainstream American past values, and the race-based assumptions reaching into the American future.
- Business opportunities propelled by their race, controlled by the state, local, and federal executive orders, laws, regulations.
- Public policies are mandating race-based inclusion and participation as requirements.
- Equal access to business opportunities set aside for the company and owner on race- and gender-designated zones on the business playing field.

Finally, race-based assumptions exist in America, and they become the throttle that propels assumptions and situational cues and the harness that affect the African American entrepreneurs' journey. This study on African American entrepreneurship characterizes a contemporary perspective on the subject. It reflects the voices of everyday entrepreneurs on a quest to live the American dream in present-day America.

References

Ellison, R. 1952. *Invisible Man*, 3. New York, NY: Random House.

Nixon, R. March 5, 1969. "Executive Order 11458—Prescribing Arrangements for Developing and Coordinating a National Program for Minority Business Enterprise." *The American Presidency Project*, Online by G. Peters, and J.T. Woolley. http://presidency.ucsb.edu/ws/?pid=6047t5

CHAPTER 2

Research Overview and Context

Research is the highest form of adoration.
—Pierre Teilhard de Chardin

Over the course of four years, the authors interviewed African American entrepreneurs throughout the United States of America. This section highlights the inherent characteristics of the African American entrepreneur's experience and reflection of owning and operating a business in mainstream America as well as the key themes in the conversations with the African American entrepreneurs.

Additionally, themes are expanded on to illustrate issues that are considered necessary by African American entrepreneurs when conducting business in contemporary mainstream America.

The Entrepreneurial Context

Entrepreneurs are defined as innovators with a creative idea and the ability to communicate the concept to a team of stakeholders (Kaplan 2007). According to Bhide (2000), entrepreneurship is often romanticized, and a Hollywood version of the economy and this is just not the case. Thus, the definition of an entrepreneur has evolved as the surrounding economic structures have become more involved. These definitions dominate the perspective in entrepreneurial programs. Social learning history and entrepreneurial strategies in the African American community teach them the necessity of innovation because they must overcome the obstacles and resist the pressure placed on their businesses by the political and business environments as well as the society in general.

Rachmawan et al. (2015) perceive entrepreneurship as a process of creating something different by devoting the necessary time and effort, assuming the accompanying financial, psychic, and social risk, and receiving the resulting monetary rewards and personal satisfaction. Consequently, to understand the African American entrepreneurs today one must also understand their past as well as how that history has been translated and used during the present time.

Ogbu (1995) underscores the importance of considering interpretations and consequences. Watkins (2013) notes that people of the same race but located in different countries manifested unusual ability and achievement levels according to some measures. In the book, *Eminent Educators: Studies in Intellectual Influence*, Berude (2000) argues that cultural differences alone cannot account for differences in minority education since some minority communities do quite well, and others do not. Also, he sees that in some cases groups of people of the same race but located in different countries manifested unusual ability and achievement levels according to some measures. The conceptual frame of the African American is accepted. The framework furthers the notion that the African American's status as a descendant of the involuntary migrant compromises their ability to exercise options without complications. The African American entrepreneurs' new presence requires an exploration through the lens of inclusion and duality.

The cause and effect must be placed in time, and the cause must precede the effects temporally. According to Dilthey (1980), each new present gives us a potentially new past. The translation of history for the moment in no way affects the truth of what has occurred in the past, nor does it change the effects of the past. Controlling people and events based on inaccurate knowledge of the history cannot continue over a prolonged period.

The authors examined many entrepreneurial theories embraced by mainstream America and other small business development programs and scholarly research to map out steps, processes, and strategies for entrepreneurial development. Notable differences were observed from the findings of this study.

According to Ogbu (1978), Americans could be divided into "voluntary minorities. They are groups of immigrants who chose to come to the United States and their descendants versus 'involuntary' or 'caste-like' minorities (descendants of groups of persons who found themselves in the United States, or under United States jurisdiction, against their will)." Ogbu (1996) further argued that "involuntary minorities" often adopted an "oppositional identity" to the mainstream culture in response to a glass ceiling imposed or maintained by mainstream American society on the job-success of their parents and others in their communities. Status as an involuntary minority entrepreneur contributes to the African American entrepreneur's adoption of an "oppositional identity" (Anzaldua 2015).

In trying to analyze involuntary minority entrepreneurs, the authors learned the value of the surrounding factors such as their personal and business networks, education, and family. Lynch and Hanson (2004) found that, for entrepreneurs of color, the family unit is valued and is of primary importance in life. Limitations exist regarding parental role models and education. The Bureau of Labor Statistics shows that some self-employed African Americans grew by 5.7 percent in contrast to the 3.4 decrease by whites (Peck 2012). African Americans tend to be motivated by using skills, venture creation, control over life, and achievement of the desired lifestyle. The 100 Urban Entrepreneurs, New York, promote, mentor, and celebrate African American self-employment. African American businesses increased by 34.5 percent between 2007 and 2012, totaling 2.8 million. About 95 percent are sole proprietors, 1.1 million operated in health care and social assistance (Blackdemographics.com 2017). African American men are one-third more likely to be self-employed as compared to white men (Fairlie 1999).

W.E.B. Dubois reminds African Americans:

In the midst of life and deeds it is easy to have endurance and strength and determination, but Thy Word, O Lord, teaches us, that this is not enough to bring good to the world to bring happiness and the worthier success. (Rust College 2017)

For this, we must endure the end—learn to finish things—to take them to the accomplishment and full fruition. Not be content with plans, ambitions, and resolves; with part of a message or part of an education, but be set and determined to fulfill the promise and complete the task and secure the full training (The African American Lectionary 2017).

The surrounding factors are grounded by gravity, and they cannot be diverted. The African American entrepreneur has been challenged by the legal system, the culture, financial institutions. In many studies, African American entrepreneurs have been shown to be constrained by business factors such as access to financing, lack of customer support, lack of access to management support, and racial discrimination (Sullivan 2007; Ouellet 2007; Pages 2005; Zajonc 2003). Also, Black American business is often constrained by lack of capital and weak banking relationships, which leads to business failures (Bates 1996).

As Ralph Ellison's (1952) narrator reminds us in *Invisible Man*, black discourse is derived from our paradoxical visibility and invisibility to most white Americans. In the words of Ellison's nameless narrator, "When they [whites] approach me [the nonwhite other], they see only my surroundings, themselves, or figments of their imagination—indeed everything and anything except me" (Bell 1987).

The African American entrepreneurs' inclusion into mainstream American business opportunities has been mapped, modeled, and prescribed by laws and regulations. The mandated minority set-aside inclusion process is consistently pushed forward and pulled backward by political and social agendas. Overtly and covertly American history has demonstrated the need for the legislation of laws and regulations. In the words of Dr. Martin Luther King Jr. (1967), "power is simply the ability to achieve the purpose." The data generated from the African American business owners indicate that lack of inclusion limits power and ability to reach the goal.

The owner of a successful construction company stated:

Everything we do in the building trades requires the understanding and cooperation of prime contractors, union workers, and 8A certification set-aside government regulations and mandates.

As the proprietor of a successful construction company in a major metropolitan city, and a migrant from the south continues the conversation he stated:

I understand the importance of the kitchen table discussions, I know I will learn when sitting down, I listen to the folks with experience in the trades and the white prime contractors, the discussion turns into a debate, and this helps make my situation on a construction site work for my company.

Detroit, a location recognized not only as one of the best places for African American entrepreneurs is also known as the home of the most powerful African American role models. According to Hiram E. Jackson, Chief Executive Officer, Real-Time Media Interim Publisher Michigan Chronicle,

> We do not hear about their selfless acts every day as they quietly go about the business of leading particular companies. (Shea, 2013)

Issues Confronting African American Entrepreneurship

Entrepreneurial success requires continuous reflection upon past experiences because they help in interpreting situational cues in a manner that leads to awareness of the opportunity, challenge, or even risks associated with the day-to-day operations of the business. Long-term success for the African American entrepreneur requires active interaction between mainstream America and the African American communities. They must revisit the past experiences and social history of African American business owners.

The African American entrepreneur's environments are littered with assumptions and stereotypes that further contribute to separation and segregation of the entrepreneurial race-designated business zone. The complicated, time-consuming, frequently crippling certification process to be classified as a minority business and 51 percent owner is one example. Another is the unintentional boomerang effect of their associated race-based status. Most of the entrepreneurs interviewed showed an awareness of these and other stumbling stones.

The entrepreneurial definitions define the entrepreneur as a "calculated risk taker." African American entrepreneurs have nothing to risk when they start a business enterprise because they are often underemployed, unemployed with less than average median net worth and per capita income. They become entrepreneurs because the surrounding environment often forces their lifestyle into a survival mode. They also have an entrepreneurial history that began in Africa and remained a part of their lifestyle during and after slavery.

Entrepreneurship is a part of African American social history. They instinctively calculate risk because they want to survive. Unlike mainstream American entrepreneurs, African Americans, limited access to capital is the result of the lingering effects of race-based discrimination by financial institutions and race-based assumptions and stereotypes. Therefore, African Americans do not have access to capital. However, the lack of access to capital is something their social learning history teaches them to incorporate into their way of lifestyle. The African Americans' social learning history teaches them to "make do" and become innovative as a necessary survival skill. Rotter's (1942) Social Learning theory can be applied to the strategies that African Americans use to their lack of capital. The data generated also indicates that they incorporate the empirical law of effect, which states that people are motivated to seek out current stimulation, or reinforcement, and to avoid unpleasant stimulation. Rotter's theory underscores the need to understand both the individual and his or her life history of learning and experiences and the "environment," that is, those stimuli that the person is aware of and responding to into account.

The Civil Rights Act of 1964 and the Equal Employment Opportunity Commission (Archives.gov 2017) provided a foundation for change. The subsequent laws supporting minorities entered our vocabulary as a mandate for reducing discrimination based on race and ethnicity in America (Kauffman.org 2017). However, the term has been interpreted and implemented differently in each setting. Unfortunately, the mandate and time are frequently considered a reverse discrimination or quota systems for second-class businesses that are not qualified to participate equally with majority-owned firms. This viewpoint has been forcefully put forward by some African American entrepreneurs who had been receiving contracts they fear losing with the new competition. The minority set-aside programs, regulations, and legislation at the federal, state, and local levels that followed on the heels of the race desegregation movement are not embraced without complications and challenges. Race and ethnicity continue as the primary factor economic parity differences. The adverse effects of slavery and reconstruction and the transformation and conversion impact that requires legislation and ongoing initiatives such as the Civil Rights Act, Affirmative Action, minority set-aside and diversity programs are expected to be understood and accepted as the national effort to provide opportunities for economic inclusion of African Americans. However, the silent social and political codes supported by prejudices, stereotypes, pessimism, lack of race-based transformation and conversions, and the race-based assumptions reinforced by mainstream Americans play a prominent role in the interactions between mainstream Americans and African American entrepreneurs.

The unspoken codes are frequently culturally driven by stereotypes, negative and reactive interfaces between entrepreneurs, and an economy locked into a downward spiral, that results in fierce competition between competitors. The unspoken codes remain broken. The silent-unspoken codes identify minority business set-aside opportunities for African American business enterprises, as a premium, not a necessity to overcome limited access to business opportunities. The racially and ethnically based social and political codes provide a pathway for mainstream Americans to quietly circumvent stereotypes, and lack of inclusion and access to small business opportunities.

City of Richmond v. J.R. Croson Co. considered affirmative action in the context of government "set-asides": programs. The government that set aside a specified percentage of government contract dollars for minority business enterprises. Rejecting the argument that racial set-asides might be justified as a remedy for past societal discrimination, the Court held that such programs are only justified as a remedy for past discrimination by the government entity adopting the set-asides. Croson, and a subsequent case involving a federal set-aside program (*Adarand Constructors v. Pena* (1995)) make clear that all racial classifications will be subject to the strict scrutiny test requiring demonstration of a compelling state interest and use of classifications narrowly tailored to further that interest. Moreover, I want to use this case of April 1999, when the Ohio Supreme Court, led by Chief Justice Thomas Moyer, voted unanimously that the set-aside provision on goods and services House Bill 584 was constitutional.

A federal judge had disallowed the construction set-aside provisions at an earlier time. The Civil Rights Act of 1964, subsequently set the framework for legislated initiatives that mandated equal access for African American entrepreneurs to mainstream American economic resources. It opened up doors for inclusion, as well as new business opportunities.

The Fourteenth Amendment "Part II." What *Brown v. Board of Education* should have said: the nation's top legal experts rewrite America's landmark civil rights decision (Pusey 1963, Balkin 2001). Annotation 18—Fourteenth Amendment: Section 1—Rights Guaranteed: Equal Protection of the Laws: Scope and application state action (Findlaw 2017) guarantees that no state shall "deny to any person within its jurisdiction the equal protection of the laws" and has been used to challenge and strictly scrutinize and limit the laws enacted to assist minority businesses.

- The minority set-aside programs attempt to correct the discriminatory practices. The practices are often the underlying issues associated with discrimination. The pervasive, silent-unspoken social and political race and ethnic-negative stereotype codes for exclusion that are accepted and practiced by mainstream America lead to the economic exclusion of African Americans. In 1995, Supreme Court Justice Clarence Thomas Text of *Adarand Constructors, Inc. v. Peña*, 515 U.S. 200 (1995) (Justia 2017).
- U.S. Commission on Civil Rights, Federal Procurement After *Adarand* (USCCR.gov 2017).
- *Adarand Constructors, Inc. v. Peña* Case (Oyez.org 1994).

This case cast the deciding vote in the Supreme Court on affirmative action and argued for the immediate end to affirmative action.

African American entrepreneurs' access to economic inclusion is the most crucial element in the development of economically sustainable African American communities and families. The Fourteenth Amendment to the Constitution was adopted on July 9, 1868, as one of the reconstruction amendments (Boundless.com 2017). Federal government contract stipulates that at least 23 percent of federal contract dollars should go to small businesses, 5 percent of which need to be small disadvantaged businesses (SBA 2017).

The Citizens Clause provides a broad definition of citizenship that overruled the decision in *Dred Scott V. Sanford* in 1857 (Pbs.org 2017). *Dred Scott v. Sandford*, 60 U.S. 393 (1857), also known as the *Dred Scott case*, was a landmark decision by the United States Supreme Court on U.S. labor law and constitutional law (Fehenbacher 1978). It held that "a negro, whose ancestors were imported into [the U.S.], and sold as slaves which ruled that the black could not be citizens of the United States resulting in a century-old stereotype that was not eliminated by legislation and mandates." The silent-unspoken race and ethnic, social code for exclusion directed toward African Americans continue to limit their access to economic inclusion and the development of economically sustainable businesses by African Americans. These race-based assumptions are rooted in the realities of being an African American in this country as well as social, cultural norms that set the standards by which the entrepreneur has chosen to conduct him or herself.

These assumptions are intrusive external elements that are rooted in the social learning history through which the African American entrepreneur has learned to interpret assumptions and perceptions and developed the needed awareness to respond in a way that is beneficial rather than reactive. The race-based throttle many African American entrepreneurs use to frame responses to mainstream American's control of opportunities within designated enterprise zones results in the unintended consequence of internal pressures directly associated with their designation as minority business owner. The resulting scenario becomes one of exclusion rather than economic inclusion.

Environmental Influence

The exclusion of African Americans from economic inclusion is seen clearly through the experiences of typical African American entrepreneurs. An Ohio company interviewed was a third-generation conglomerate of family-owned businesses in the retail, wholesale, service, and real estate industries, with second- and third-generation owners having college degrees. Three percent of the third-generation principal owners responding to the questionnaire and subsequently interviewed shared concerns. They lost some opportunities through the lack of access interface with the majority community and thus have still been small while *"we had opportunities to grow to a large size or even bigger company."* This owner's viewpoint provides insight into unintended consequences of the race-based throttle.

- *Corson* Case and *Adarand v. Pena* in 1996 (Justia 2017) *Text of Adarand Constructors, Inc. v. Peña*, 515 U.S. 200 (1995).
- U.S. Commission on Civil Rights, Federal Procurement After *Adarand* (USCCR.gov 2017).
- *Adarand Constructors, Inc. v. Peña* Case (Justia 2017).

The cases challenged the legitimacy of the minority set-aside program. The court challenges to the legislation and mandates combined with the downward spiral of the economy, and the perceptions and stereotypes of mainstream America that question the capabilities of minority entrepreneurs associated with mainstream America's sociocultural continuation of silent codes for the race and ethnic, economic exclusion.

Attitudes and Expectations

The African American woman's entrepreneurial experiences are ignored. The expectations for African American women are different. As entrepreneurs, they have been expected to assimilate into the "mainstream American woman's" perspective of gender while maintaining their "roots" in the African American culture. At the same time, African American women are outsiders looking in at mainstream American because of their race. The experience of the owner of a security firm demonstrates this. In her interview, she states:

We are a full-service firm with over 25 years of the security and investigative industry. Our primary product is background employment investigations, ongoing and post-employment levels, other services workers compensation, employee theft, identity theft, tenant screening, skip tracing insurance inquiries and more. The main core of our business has been to provide clients with professionally trained and supervised security personnel both armed and unarmed. We can satisfy a wide range security needs that include police protection, private investigation, special events security and staffing, alarm response, audio and video monitoring, and device detection. Our company is here to make the community safer. Our acceptance in this industry has not grown because this industry does not accept outsiders. The unions and the leaders in the industry do not want African Americans and especially women to gain access. Ethnic groups, such as the Irish silently block our participation in the industry resulting in our inability to operate and expand our business fully.

The owner of a nationally recognized public relations firm reflects the companies' efforts to gain contracts as a prime contractor or subcontractor/joint venture partner with majority firms. However, the requirements for bonding, the expense of post-production video equipment, the access to capital and project bonding requirements limited the female-minority businesses issues of color and gender.

She was classified based on race and subcategorized by gender. The designated playing fields classify her progress and the patterns by the industry's race-based assumptions and stereotypes. According to the entrepreneur's assessment of opportunities, because of the race and gender-based set-asides there seems to be no limit to access to opportunities on the set-aside playing fields. The owner made inroads into previously uncharted waters for an African American female-owned business. However, according to the owner, this was not an easy journey. This owner operated her company in an industry dominated by mainstream America. She shared how her social history and cultural traditions was rooted in survival and overcoming obstacles.

As another example, a third-generation owner of a stellar construction company shared the same reflection with the story of other successful construction trade, minority business owners (1) a business venture's inability to hire and keep union labor. (2) Trade labor unions did not consider collaboration with a construction trade business owned by an African American priority, without the mandates for inclusion impacting the bottom-line of the mainstream American company, (3) access to the unions for the workforce in compliance with regulations. Thus, his business could not obtain lucrative major construction contracts on a project designated as union-only building trades.

Social and economic discrimination through "silent exclusion codes" manifest in exclusionary practices generated by mainstream American's efforts to continue the control of resources according to the interviewees.

Access to Resources

The ability of an entrepreneur to access resources has an impact on the business enterprise.

When an African American business person (1) attempts to access traditional capital from financial institutions (2) utilize government-sponsored loan programs for small business owners, regardless of gender, they are limited by restrictions that do not apply to majority owners, (3) deal with a lower pool of qualified professional, skilled, and the trade union workers in industries that are dominated by the unions who have systematically excluded them and (4) access procurement opportunities with government agencies, regulated mandates, restrict and challenge the owner's sustainability. Additionally, publicly funded technical assistance is both limited by state, service restrictions and community social activism political agendas and sub and prime contractor plans and opportunities with Fortune 500 corporation. Moreover, the silent-unspoken code of discrimination and the capacity for majority multinational firms to address limited minority entrepreneurial involvement through internal diversity programs.

The owner of a tree removal company stated:

I do not know how to strategize and put the paperwork together. All I know is how to work and take down the trees. It takes a supervisor, two grounds men, and a tree trimer to take down a tree. I need equipment like more saddles, more work ropes, stump grinding machine, a bucket truck, I also need a crane. The entrepreneur stated, "banks will not lend money to me."

This systematic silent discrimination, race-based assumptions of mainstream America and the willingness of politicians to promote an agenda contrary to African American business owners is the fuel that feeds the throttle always holding the African American entrepreneur in a designated trade zone over which he or she has the right control. When further questioned by the authors, the owner responded:

> *Will I be able to establish my business without collapsing within a two-year period? I just need someone to guide me and direct me to the right path on what I need to do for my business. The big concern; insurance policies play a significant role in my company; safety procedures are number one; so I need a lot of different kinds of help. I am looking for that right person to take me in the right direction.*

The development of strategies that include education and mentors from mainstream American business owners in similar industries are needed for economic inclusion. It is the only way to ensure the development of sustainable economies in the African American community. The historical perspective has provided the backdrop for inclusion and economic integration. However, the social and political codes for exclusion driven by race-based assumptions have successfully blocked access for African American entrepreneurs to economic integration. African American entrepreneurs systematically reflected on their need for financial independence and the discontinuance of rationing economic business opportunities.

The stories shared during interviews support the need for plans to eliminate the "silent- unspoken code" and assumptions about African American entrepreneurs. The silence of the social system directed toward African Americans continues to limit their inclusion in the development of economically viable businesses.

A contractor returning to the school system as a teacher in a vocational high school after owning a housing redevelopment company stated:

> *I am the President of a residential non-union construction company. We perform construction work in the areas of drywall, framing, exterior and interior painting and roofing and siding, which is the re-carpentry work. We also have done some light electrical work and some light plumbing work. My primary need right now is for a mentor to assist me in the administration marketing and bidding. I want a proj-*

ect that comes with the opportunity for management and scheduling, those my most essential needs are not. My strengths, I have a good management team with excellent construction trades that include everything for both inside and outside rehabilitation and new construction. I also have two other partners who are working with me. I am a good boss and leader (does not indicate why the owner returned to school).

This interviewee returned to complete his undergraduate degree in Ohio from the military in the early 2000s as a wounded warrior, describing his background he says:

I saw combat service as a member of the Army after serving as a reserve officer while attending college; I had done some landscaping before I was called to active duty to help me support myself while I attended college and to help with the family business after college. My mother was a single parent. I presume I could be described as a semi-entrepreneur because I sold my services as an independent contractor to my extended family, community and social network. I worked during the week and every weekend and breaks from school. The business became away for my family to survive.

This interview illustrates that one of the pressing needs of the African American entrepreneur is support and mentoring in the administrative and management aspects of running and growing a business enterprise and the recruitment of employees and succession planning. As mainstream American entrepreneurs struggle to find ways to eliminate deeply rooted invisible biases, many African American entrepreneurs have presented them with excellent opportunities to provide support while creating informal relationships that are often essential for the development of sustainable businesses. Non-African American business self-employed owners take a risk, sharing ability and knowledge that aid African American entrepreneurs in creating economically viable businesses within communities without boundaries. The benefit for the African American mentors is evident. However, the prospective mentor benefit is equally valuable as he/she now becomes the vehicle through which separation and segregation in the entrepreneurial world give way to the gradual development of a truly leveled business zone whose throttle is not race-based. Legislation, regulation, and mandates help everyone in the community. It should be noted this entrepreneur returned home from the war as a wounded veteran. He immediately activated his business and enrolled in graduate school.

Role of Family, Role Models, and Mentors

The authors posed questions relating to the family, role models, and mentors. The responses below reflect the impact or lack thereof of family, role models, and mentors.

In one interview, the importance of household, extended families, business networks, and relationships was emphasized.

Interviewer: What is your business?

Response: *We are a commercial heating and ventilation air conditioning (HVAC union) company. We specialize in new and expansion construction. We are a national leader in the delivery of high commercial and public building and maintenance projects. Our company is set apart by its distinctive safety record, quality of work, on-time project completion, on schedule and within budget. Our history of being a prime contractor has resulted in long-term relationships with both top construction contractors and Fortune 500 companies.*

Another owner described his business as:

A company providing services in all phases of plastering through the interior and exterior, stuffed gold, spray on fireproofing, and we are getting more into the phase of carpentry and drywall too. We have been in existence since 1994 and have done quite a few projects through strong networks.

Interviewer: What do you think are the essential skills needed for African Americans to succeed in America? Also, what personal attitudes do you think are essential?

Response: *Relationships with members of my family, someone who has walked the talk before and shortened the long distance to success and steadiness saying instead of doing it this way they say most of the time you need to do it this way.*

Instead of taking five-years to do something my way, now I know how to cut it down to eight months to a year. I think that is what I need, someone from my family or married or dating someone in business to help me. Also, someone who has contacts to put me in place, let me show my ability and what I can do as an owner.

Interviewer: What are your pressing needs?

Response: *The most urgent need today is probably mentoring and collaboration with majority companies to assist along the process. From what I have seen a lot of other smaller companies that's what they get when they are involved with more well-known businesses. The more successful company helps them walk through the process, and it helps them stay profitable and helps keep them alive. The most important thing is staying busy every day and in keeping your employees working and keeping the doors open.*

Interviewer: What are your strengths and weaknesses?

Response: *My strengths are I believe that whomever I am doing business with will understand I am someone they want to do business with me. I think those are some significant components that your client can trust you. I think my weakness is that sometimes we get too many jobs at once and they all flow together somehow, and we get all out the schedule, and once that happens, and not having the assessable workforce and capital to control all those projects that have come at that given time. So those are some of the things that we are working on and trying not to let happen, but sometimes those things happen.*

Interviewer: Do you currently have a role model?

Response: *Yes, I have an excellent role model. A retired businessperson, he is also active in the community, I think I have done much networking. I have met a lot of interesting people like I said they helped me a lot to build my center and I gained much real ability regarding that, such as financial planning, insurance planning. So, regarding a lot of general business things, it has been an incredible experience for me, and I do continue to remain very active. I think African Americans must network across racial boundaries.*

In another interview, a retired successful former professional ball-player emphasized the need to follow the rules and be a part of a team. He stated:

You gotta know how to work from your strengths, how to play as a member of a team, how to network effectively and how to build a winner by surrounding yourself with the best people while playing on a field that is not level, filled with dumb rules and always changing. First, you must get your foot in the door and then you must play to win by figuring out the rules, regulations, and procedures. Next, you must compete to be the best against the other businesses while just being yourself, you know straight with everybody and work with other guys.

Another interview cited the need to manage with minimal resources and promptly gather information and support. The entrepreneur shared personal views in this manner:

I am a photojournalist with a history of 20 years in the venture. Through photography, I create intimate portraits that communicate a message, tell a story, and by the viewer to come into the visual environment. My photography business will photograph private or public events, take pictures of individuals and groups in the studio or on location. I am a single parent of a daughter. My mission is to "tell your story through photography." I attended college briefly, and I started working as a freelance photographer. I picked up a camera, and I started my business. I am mobile, and I will take any pictures. Most of my business is with the African American community and corporation actively engaged in minority inclusion. I do not have a professional personal network. I network with the community through my photography business. Everyone knows I can ask for information or support. I have rarely been invited to shoot events outside of the African American community or events featuring African Americans. As a photographer, I make my living selling photographic services I always owe someone. My finances are a mess. I do not see my business growing because I do not have access to money. I need to buy new and better equipment. Options in the photography in this city are limited if you are black and your jobs are for the black folks. I would not recommend freelance solo business ownership in this industry if you are black in you cannot move to another city.

Diversity and Inclusion

Broadly defined, the definition of diversity refers to specific categories of human differences such as race, ethnicity, gender, sexual orientation, and disability (Bloom 2002; Muller and Parham 1998). The term implies "belonging" to a subgroup within a mainstream group. The term inclusion is based on the reality that subgroups are excluded. Inclusion redefined the concept of desegregation and equal opportunity. Diversity requires representation, and in the absence of inclusion active connection of people and, consequently, productivity and growth cannot happen (Sherbin and Rashid 2017).

One of the most significant problems facing African American entrepreneurs is the involuntary minority subgroup status and their need for diversity and inclusion that requires national and local mandates. The lack of diversity and inclusion can be linked to the failure by mainstream America to include involuntary and voluntary minorities. In 2010, Senator Bob Casey (D-PA) introduced a bill aimed at protecting involuntary minority entrepreneurs. The senator said, "Especially in the current economic climate, supporting small micro-enterprise is vital to economic recovery" (Maryland.gov 2017). Roberson (2006) notes that the term inclusion is often coupled with the term *diversity* and these terms are often used interchangeably. However, they are distinctly different.

In the African American subculture, inclusion is considered necessary by American mainstream entrepreneurs. They are expected to demonstrate their ability to overcome race-based barriers in the mainstream American culture. On their journey to economic sustainability and business success, African American entrepreneurs must successfully assimilate into the mainstream America lifestyle, overcome self-filling prophecies, lower expectations, and governmental regulations as well as expectations imposed by the African American community.

A Process of Transformation

African American entrepreneurs are continuously undergoing personal, social, and business changes. The changes correspond to the societal transformations in the state, local, and federal mandates driven by mainstream America to ensure the inclusion of all ethnic and minority groups in the pursuit of the American dream. However, they also impose restrictions. Although the entrepreneurs are aware of the changes and society recognizes the need for change in viewpoints and assumptions. Through the interviews the authors conducted with the African American entrepreneurs, research was gathered exploring the balance between the subjective and the objective. The authors regularly heard the words "inclusion," "minority participation," "minority set-aside," and "equal access." Over and over, they listened to the accounts of the impact of these words that define a process developed to solve the African American entrepreneur's access to equal business opportunities. The authors have seen the day-to-day operations of the African American and mainstream American ventures, the local and national economic impact of these investments on the community. References to these words did not surprise the authors. The constant need to overcome the challenges facing African American entrepreneurs in the United States remains a reality.

Although mainstream American entrepreneurs have contested the necessity for race-based inclusion and mandates for minority businesses, through a review of the responses given, it became apparent that the public laws, regulations, and orders for enhanced options for African American business owners remain a necessity.

Understanding the role that social networks and connections with professional and business communities play in the success of African American entrepreneurs was reported as a positive predictor of success. The authors noted community networks linked to their lifestyle such as fraternal organizations, and churches participation is an integral part of their lives. Therefore, the authors considered church participation and fraternal organizations as a culturally based resource among African American entrepreneurs who provide a network of supporters for the entrepreneurs.

Access to private mainstream American golf clubs was overcome by the founding of the National Association of Negro Golfers (NNGA) in 1965. This organization mentors African Americans and provides an opportunity to network with business owners. NNGA has a history of economic, education, and business support in their community and the majority of them ultimately become leaders in their professions and as politicians.

Several entrepreneurs recognized the prejudices, intolerances in the mainstream American community and the opportunity for social networking opportunities linked to their business was a significant factor in the success of their business. About 80 percent of the respondents expressed a sense of isolation from mainstream American business networking opportunities.

The extent of negativity and disappointment was alarming. A successful owner of an HVAC company stated that he experienced the feeling that *"they do not want to be bothered with us;" as a result, he believed that the mainstream American business community and the trade unions adversely affect his ability to grow his business. Some respondents reported that they feel they are unfairly judged because of their race during networking events.* Some reported racial hostility or lack of inclusion on the part of some organization and privately owned golf and tennis clubs, one owner was quoted as saying he was *"racially" profiled on the golf course in addition to his qualifications to operate a business. Others reported that mainstream American entrepreneurs reached out to them frequently, while others challenge the inclusion requirements and expressed experienced hostility.*

A sense of exclusion was felt. Most of the interviewees said they are prepared educationally and financially for membership in private clubs. Traditionally, these are the primary location for business networking events. However, they are not invited to join private membership organizations, resulting in the limited number of African American members. The number of college-educated entrepreneurs actively engaged in playing golf or tennis suggests that a considerable number are prepared to become members. It is unclear from available data what the rate of membership is.

Most of the profiles and follow-up interviews share the strengths and challenges of associated minority certifications and opportunities mandated by legislation and regulations. A communication installation business owner stated:

Minority certifications guarantee all our work, and our customers love it. Our challenges are our cash flow. Our telecommunications products are a structural cadence, cell phones, and virtual communication systems. We have been in business for twenty-five years now. We have many certifications and install communication-systems, so we have small as well as significant minority and majority businesses as some of the customers we serve and our clientele list.

A janitorial supply company owner stated:

We literally can become a one-stop shop for some different industrial end-users so far as their chemicals, cleaning, and safety items. We also provide ice melts, and now we are selling office supplies. So, a purchaser could pick up the phone and order everything they need right from us and represent multiple suppliers were and always in stock. One of our biggest weaknesses is, as I said before, business-related networks of professionals with the majority business owners.

A young, successful aerospace systems engineer and business owner who graduated from two Ivy League universities was asked why he had not registered as a minority engineering firm. He quickly responded by saying:

It is better for the corporation not know my race. If they knew I was an African American engineer, they would question my company and the quality of my service. I operate incognito; the client does not know I am African American.

This African American small business owner realized that federal legislation generates terms of engagement that will create assumptions about the proprietor's ability. These assumptions are magnified in the technology industry. The owner believes that race will damage or hinder the company's ability to grow one's business. He understands from social learning and elder's stories the importance of a dual life as a supplier of services to technology corporations.

Additionally, this entrepreneur shared concerns about the mandated rules of engagement for business opportunities and massive amounts of regulations for inclusion that generate stick-throwing reactions from mainstream America. The rules often cause institutional racism and limit interactive communication with mainstream American peers in the aerospace industry, especially those doing business on government contracts. It should be noted that this engineer is actively engaged as a mentor to other African American engineers and passionately engages in social justice community programs serving the underserved African American community. He closes the interview stating:

"Education and ability are not all the African American entrepreneur needs to develop and maintain a small business in America" We have undocumented industry success in America We need to remember the stories we were told by business owners in our community.

Since literature on the topic of African American small business owners was varied, the authors conducted in-person, one-on-one interviews, and reviewed materials written about African American entrepreneurs. It was not feasible to interview all the successful African American entrepreneurs in America, so the authors reached out to African American entrepreneurs they could reach.

Other participants in the study emphasized the duality of their business and lifestyle and the resulting boomerang effect. As their companies developed, both the business and the entrepreneur/business owner advanced, with the changes occurring in both their social and business environments. The business owner's social history provided him/her with an organizational frame for duality. Most of the owners did not grow up with a social history lacking in care and values. As entrepreneurs, they developed an understanding of the harness controlling the chain of events that joined the inequities to their social status, race, and ethnicity, and those that generated the requirements for minority business owners' access to opportunities with and through mainstream America.

Impact of Social History

Biases continue to exist. These preferences are deeply rooted, invisible, and difficult to eliminate. Many people have personal viewpoints and opinion about the respective roles of the minority set-aside rulings that are designed to level the business zone for African American entrepreneurs. These views influence attitudes toward African American entrepreneurs and the new mandate for economic inclusion.

Many mainstream American small business owners believe that the equal opportunity and inclusion programs, referendums, laws, and regulations provide an unfair advantage to minorities. Therefore, they cannot and do not support the strategies for their economic inclusion unless it affects their bottom line.

Social learning history can be a barrier. However, it can be overcome. A survey respondent spent 19 years in prison and became a practicing Nations of Gods and Earths, also known as Five Percent Nation or the Five Percenters (Splcenter.org 2017).

Need for Economic Inclusion Interviewee

A middle-aged man lobbied for support from the state to learn heating, ventilation, and air conditioning regulations and installations while incarcerated. When released from prison he attempted to become an apprentice in the HVAC union. He recognized the union did not allow ex-offenders to become members. The Mayor of a Midwest City negotiated a variation in the HVAC membership requirements with local union leaders. As a result, the man became a qualified master plumber. He accepted his past mistake and the consequences as he launched his business. He worked long hours, discounted the stereotypes, and emphasized the duality of his social and business worlds. As an African American male ex-offender, he traveled the social status and race-based designated winding road in social, family, and business environments. As an African American man attempting to "live the American dream," he became an entrepreneur. He took part in a small business program customized to support African American male business owners. The program for African American men helped launch his business. He learned how to secure minority-set aside contracts and achieve realistic objectives. He strengthens his ability to reflect and connect his wisdom from his experiences to re-enter society. Through his reflections, he developed the tools needed to shape and negotiate his entrance into the world of entrepreneurship and re-entry into society. Twenty years later, he is a success, a contributor to the economic sustainability of a metropolitan community, the owner of a home in the inner city. He is a single parent of an honor student preparing to attend college. This man is a storyteller. He enjoys sharing his journey with others to help them overcome situations unique to African American males and ex-offenders.

Politicians, social activists, religious representatives, and minority entrepreneurs lobbied for economic inclusion to earn equal opportunities as those granted to mainstream American people in the business. This scenario leads to the stabilization of the African American ex-offenders access to apprenticeships and union membership community. Economic inclusion for African Americans in urban, low-income communities can be elusive especially in areas experiencing high unemployment. The report "One Nation Underemployed: Jobs Rebuild America" (Cbslocal.com 2017) noted that the underemployment rate for black workers at 20.5 percent is significantly higher than the 11.8 percent for white workers. Underemployment is defined as those who are jobless or working part-time jobs but desiring full-time work (CBS 2017). The report also indicated that blacks are twice as likely as whites to be unemployed. The unemployment rate for blacks was 12 percent in February 2015, compared with 5.8 percent for whites. Until those with the power to change the system and the race and gender-based distribution of wealth are at the table, no substantive progress will be made. Owners included in the interviews have developed and conducted discussion roundtables and economic development organizations throughout America.

African American entrepreneurs are actively lobbying to mainstream American leaders. They established business partnerships with mainstream American companies to influence key decision makers to reach out to their peers. They recognize that if the minority business is to gain equal access to mainstream American small business opportunities, then this begins with active efforts to eliminate assumptions concerning the qualifications of African Americans based on the interactive dialogue between peers.

The entrepreneurs viewed collaboration as a systematic process that required all participants to identify scalable differences, needs, and similarities outside of the laws and mandates for inclusion that focus on solutions and the application of interventions without legislative orders and legislation for inclusion.

A randomly selected group of entrepreneurs were asked to discuss the challenges they faced when building their business for race-based listing and how they overcame the challenges. The interviews included a discussion about the stressful business events the entrepreneur encountered and links to decision and assumptions concerning the quality of their business operation and race. An examination of the responses indicated that the boomerang effect of race was present and that biased assumptions must continually be recognized.

Harquail (2010) stated that "treating all types of differences as though they were the same is damaging both to the individual, organizational member and to an organization's progress toward inclusivity." A difference based on race in America continues. Discrimination and segregation remain at the forefront of economic and social inclusion by mainstream America.

Another group interviewed consisted of community leaders, former pro ball players, small business owners, and professional service providers. They answered the questions and highlighted the need to provide support for the magnitude of economic development and job creation issues. The race-based effect of the boomerang from the golf course to the boardroom was six times higher than the combined impact on mainstream American small business owners' sports alumni operating in similar industries. These interviews found that African Americans provided support to other African Americans through university-based programs, professional membership, and social organizations and informal networking.

The strategy developed by this group of entrepreneurs gave an anchor to economic sustainability and community leadership development. A successful African American entrepreneur is operating in the State of Ohio posted on the company website: "Expertise +Finance+ Diversity + Success." Another small business owner from this region believed in partnerships, rather than acting in a silo separating him from minority and majority entrepreneurs. The interview findings show that quite often African American company owners operate as a network of storytellers sharing their entrepreneurial journey, information, and resources.

Networking Is Essential

The ability to collaborate in social settings is essential. When was a group of business owners asked, "Are these organizations unique to African Americans or open to all races? Did they contribute to your business success?" These owners decided early on to pursue partnerships with multiracial firms to better deliver results for clients.

Porter and Kramer (2011) explored the concept of shared value and the connections of societal and economic progress and enabling socioeconomic clusters to mainstream disadvantaged residents through training and small business development opportunities. One entrepreneur interviewed is someone who would qualify for business development assistance; he was a disadvantaged urban community resident, an ex-offender, and an African American male. The designated business zone for his business generated the frameworks he needed to develop strategies to overcome the effects of the boomerang. Each stick thrown at him proposed different areas for entrepreneurial development. African American business development professionals assigned to the African American business zone were primarily concerned with the "birth" of his business. Accordingly, they stressed the importance of an effective plan of activities and milestones generated to maintain accountability of the owner. In contrast, the programs serving ex-offenders focus on social learning, social history, moral and emotional development, aggression, and dishonesty. Standing apart from business and social-psychological development is the development of social capital in a disadvantaged urban community, the need for race-based and mainstream acceptance unique to the educated and experienced entrepreneur. The owner also needs recognition for his potential as a contributor to the community, not a distracter, to the community. He quickly developed social capital by sharing his "thinking" and his ability to view his options through a personal optical lens. This entrepreneur understood the stumbling blocks, the importance of building a network of minority and majority decision makers, and how to negotiate the winding road that would result in success as an entrepreneur.

In contrast, another interviewee, founder and CEO with more than 35 years of sales and marketing experience, a bachelor's degree in economics from the nation's most prestigious universities, and an active community volunteer who was expected to maintain and grow his business, practiced duality and avoided the boomerang. His company sold business furniture and products to institutions. He is an American vendor of commercial office supplies, furniture, fixtures and other product. Based on the public law mandates he had access to opportunities. This owner, however, paid a higher price for his products because he did not own the manufacturing company, resulting in a lower profit margin, and limiting his ability to sell his product contracts because of pricing and competition with the manufacturer. While the public laws mandated access to contract opportunities, limited his options for contracts based on pricing race-based access to opportunities. The circumstances impact the growth of his business. This Ivy League-educated, successful salesperson did not own the manufacturing firm and, as a result, not owning a manufacturing company led to the boomerang effect. Race and assumptions with or without education will affect the African American business owner. When asked the question, "Are you a member of a business organization? Are these groups unique to African Americans or open to all races? Did they contribute to your business success?" He very quickly responded yes and that he was an active participant in his African American fraternity and diverse community organizations sponsored by mainstream Americans.

These interviewees came from all walks of life. Some ran established businesses, others were just starting out, and still, others inherited the business. Some were seasoned businesspeople, while others were young entrepreneurs. Some were highly educated; others were not. The interviewees were regular, real-life African American entrepreneurs in America. They shared commonalities in thinking and approaches. The idea is not to bundle together or generalize African American attitudes, but to examine whether the success strategies could also work without the public laws and executive orders.

The entrepreneurs presented in this book exist in a world linked to objects, events, and circumstances they cannot control, nor will they ever be able to monitor because they are the descendants of African American unwilling migrants who did not volunteer to migrate to America. Mainstream Americans have defined their ethnicity as a minority, and they struggle daily against biases and racial stereotypes.

Pursuit of the American Dream

The American dream—freedom, opportunity, prosperity, and upward mobility—is rooted in the American culture. The CEO of the U.S. Chamber of Commerce, Thomas J. Donohue (2012), speaking at the U.S. Chamber of Commerce event, *The State of American Business* (January 12, 2012) stated that "Immigrants come to America with great dreams for a better life and they always face significant challenges."

In the view of Michael Jordan, "I can accept failure, everyone fails at something, but I cannot accept not training." America is a haven, where ordinary men and women, armed with a dream and a willingness to take a risk and work hard, can make their dreams a reality (Reynolds 2007).

The broad acceptance of the American dream contributes to a significant number of African Americans finding their American dream as entrepreneurs. There is a reason for this. In this book, the authors bring into focus the entrepreneurial thinking of the African American entrepreneur regarding his/her understanding of their uneasy interactions with mainstream America. They each reflect on their activities as a business owner, and the roadblocks, the intersections, and gateways to success.

The drive and optimism have been evident in several interviews. The interview excerpt below is an example:

Interviewer: Can you tell us a little bit about yourself and your business?

Response: *Sure, I am the owner of a transportation company. We do small group shuttle service in the State of Ohio.*

Interviewer: What are your most pressing needs?

Response: *We need a little more capital, some garage space to store our vans and bigger office space.*

Interviewer: What are your strengths and weaknesses?

Response: *My company's strengths are that we are dependable. We like to be on time and are very professional in any job whether big or small. Our weaknesses are that we are a little too polite when people do not have the correct finances they need to pay for services. It is sometimes hard to let them know we cannot do it because they do not have the money. Sometimes, people take kindness for weakness.*

Interviewer: Do you currently have a mentor?

Response: *Yes.*

Interviewer: Is there any additional information you would like to add about yourself or your company?

Response: *We are a family owned business. My husband and I run the company, and we have been in business for three years now. It has been an uphill battle, but it is great with the help of the minority technical assistance program. It is great being introduced to new people. That has been a tremendous help because without them we could not have made it this far.*

The notion of success and the link to a family member's traditional employment and or business engagement. When asked "does anyone in your family own and operate a business?"—about 70 percent worked as an apprentice for immediate and extended family member's informal-unregistered business and formally registered business. These nonregistered informal businesses started to "make ends meet" during a phase of unemployment. Eventually, they generated additional cash resources to buy a home for their family because home mortgages in their urban community are not available.

Many of the individuals included in this book operated their business in the designated playground zone for African American entrepreneurs. The construction of the different zones on the entrepreneurial playing field is driven and controlled by mandates developed to assist and include entrepreneurs of color and women and help build sustainable businesses. The African American entrepreneurs' designated business zones are in continuous transformation processes. State, federal, and local government legislation mandates for economic inclusion mandates, lawsuits challenging the terms, social, political, historical change, growing unrest in urban communities, high-, under-, and unemployment in urban African American communities resulting in turmoil in the African American designated business zones.

The complexities of the mandates have turned into a boomerang effect. When an African American entrepreneur starts a business venture, they are required to declare their race when they formally request access to information, opportunities, and resources. Each of the entrepreneurs interviewed for this book remembers their first interaction with financial institutions, business development professionals, and organizations.

The business owners reflected on being interviewed or filling out a questionnaire, survey, or application for assistance or information. Owners discussed attempts to demonstrate their ability as entrepreneurs and their sense of powerlessness during the interactions. They each went on to discuss and respond to the questions: Did you come across any unique circumstances because of your race? Why are African American entrepreneurs different from the mainstream American business person? What challenges did African American entrepreneurs face?

The idea behind starting a business was fragmented for most of the responses to the questionnaires and during the interviews. The owners were in search of the American Dream, from business development perspectives. They are required to answer a series of questions when they registered their companies and issues concerning their race. The owners need to decide, are they going to register as an African American business entrepreneur or merely an entrepreneur? The business process requires individuals to choose to categorize themselves as different from mainstream American business owners.

In answering this question about their race, they will be expected to approach organizations, institutions, and potential business opportunities designated for minority participation. The process becomes structured by policies, rules, expectations, and current political and social transformations. The process requires the entrepreneur identify themselves as an African American. The business owners all agreed they did not have control over this process or the decision to determine their business by race. The factors the owner uses to help him/her decide to declare their race when they start a business, apply for business development assistance and business opportunities designated for minorities or identify resources will be related to social history and perceived opportunities available based on mandates for inclusion, diversity, and minority set-asides. To set out and register a business as an African American business is a challenge.

Each of the individuals interviewed experienced storytelling by elders, the continual assessment their social history, and the present status of their race in American linkages. They expressed the stories that included cultural histories linked to business ownership as key elements in their growth and expansion into their awareness of their race and the duality designated as a business owner based on race. The age of the entrepreneur, their early life experiences as an African American had an impact on their business management and strategic planning. They also share similar views about the political and social transformation and assumptions related to their race that influenced their choices of activities.

One case pertained to a marketing company owned by an African American. During the interview, the owner stated:

> *Our strengths are our certifications throughout State and the Country. Finding working capital funding, however, for major industrial projects, bank mortgages for purchases. Such as equipment, commercial property and homes are difficult for African Americans small business owners because of the continuously changing "bottom lines and race-based assumptions about the location of the business, homes, and community."*

The owners learned during that certification as a Minority Business Enterprise (MBE) are necessary to grow a healthy sustainable business. Therefore, the strategy is to develop a protective buffer for the boomerang effect for inclusion by mainstream American marketing enterprise. The opportunity to register as an MBE exists for all participants in the survey and owners selected for the random follow-up interview. The effect of the decision to register as an MBE was direct and critical in the owners' ability to build a sustainable business.

One memorable interview was with a man seeking to gain control of the mandates for minority inclusion. He maintained that self-hood (I) status as critical in building his business and the first step in successfully moving his business forward. He was a stubborn African American man supported by his wife and a mainstream American mentor. However, he was very determined to grow his business and control the playing field. This owner learned the importance of collaborations with mainstream America designed so that everyone can win.

The pursuit of the American dream is in the hearts and minds of many African American entrepreneurs; however, the mandates frequently dominate their thoughts.

References

Anzaldua, G.E. 2015. *Light in the Dark/Luz Menlo Oscuro: Rewriting Identity*. North Carolina: Duke University Press.

Archives.gov 2017. Available at https://archives.gov/education/lessons/civil-rights-act (accessed July 30, 2017).

Balkin, J. 2001. *What Brown V. Board of Education Should Have Said*. New York, NY: NYU Press.

Bates, T. 1996. "The Financial Capital Needs of Black-Owned Businesses." *The Journal of Developmental Entrepreneurship* 1, no. 1, 1–15, available at http://journals.sagepub.com/doi/abs/10.1177/1534484305285459

Berube, M.R. 2000. *Eminent Educators: Studies in Intellectual Influence*. Greenwood Press.

Bhide, A.V. 2000. *The Origin and Evolution of New Businesses*. New York, NY: Oxford University Press.

Blackdemographics.com 2017. *Black-Owned Businesses*, available at http://blackdemographics.com/economics/black-owned-businesses/ (accessed July 27, 2017).

Boundless.com 2017, available at https://courses.lumenlearning.com/boundless-politicalscience/ (accessed July 27, 2017).

Brophy, A. 2015. "Antislavery Women and the Origins of American Jurisprudence." *Texas Law Review* 94, no. 1, p. 115.

Cbslocal.com 2017. Available at http://washington.cbslocal.com/2014/04/03/urban-league-underemployment-rate-for-african-american-workers-is-20-5-percent/ (accessed July 27, 2017).

Cornell Law 2017. *Supreme Court Text*, available at https://law.cornell.edu/supremecourt/text/411/677 (accessed July 27, 2017).

Dilthey, W. 1980. *The Hermeneutic Approach to the Study of History and Culture*. Netherlands: Springer.

Dilley, R. 1992. "Contesting Markets L A General Introduction to Market, Ideology, Imagery, and Discourse." In *Contesting Markets: Analyses of Ideology, Discourse, and Practice*, ed. R. Dilley. Edinburgh: Edinburgh University Press.

Donohue, T.J. 2012. *The State of American Business 2012*, available at https://uschamber.com/speech/state-american-business-2012-address-thomas-j-donohue-president-ceo-us-chamber-commerce (accessed July 30, 2012).

Dubois, W.E.B. 1898. *The Negro in Business*. Atlanta: Atlanta University.

Ebony Magazine. 2014. "Facing the Facts, the State of Race in America" December, p. 106.

EEOC.GOV 2017. Available at https://eeoc.gov/laws/statutes/titlevii.cfm (accessed July 30, 2017).

Ellison, R. 1952. *Invisible Man*, 3. New York, NY: Random House.

Fairlie, R.W. 1999. "The Absence of the African American Owned Business: An Analysis of the Dynamics of Self-Employment." *Journal of Labor Economics* 17, no. 1, pp. 80–109.

Fairlie, R.W. 2004. "Recent Trends in Ethnic and Racial Business Ownership." *Small Business Economics* 23, no. 3, pp. 203–18.

Fehrenbacher, D.E. 1978. *The Dred Scott Case: Its Significance in American Law and Politics.* New York, NY: Oxford.

Findlaw 2017. *Amendment 14 Annotation 18*, available at http://constitution. findlaw.com/amendment14/annotation18.html (accessed July 30, 2017).

Harquail, C.V., and A.W. King. 2010. "Construing Organizational Identity: The Role of Embodied Cognition." *Organization Studies* 31, no. 12, pp. 1619–48.

Hout, M., and H. Rosen. 2000. "Self-Employment, Family Background, and Race." *The Journal of Human Resource* 35, no. 4, pp. 670–92.

Justia 2017. Available at https://supreme.justia.com/cases/federal/us/515/200/case.html (accessed July 30, 2017).

Kaplan, J.M. 2007. *Patterns of Entrepreneurship.* USA: Wiley India Pvt. Ltd.

Kauffman.org 2017. *Research Compilation on Race and Entrepreneurship*, available at http://kauffman.org/what-we-do/resources/kauffman-compilation-research-on-race-and-entrepreneurship (accessed July 27, 2017).

King, M.L. 1967. "Where Do We Go from Here?" Annual Report Delivered at the 11th convention of the Southern Christian Leadership Conference, August 16 Atlanta, GA, available at http://www-personal.umich.edu/~gmarkus/MLK_WhereDoWeGo.pdf (accessed July 30, 2017).

Lee, M.S., E.G. Rogoff, and A.N. Puryear. 1996. "Black Entrepreneurship: It Has the Past, and It Can Have a Future." *The Entrepreneurial Executive* 1, no. 2, pp. 1–9.

Lynch, E.W., and M.J. Hanson, eds. 2004. *Developing Cross-Cultural Competence: A Guide for Working with Children and their Families.* Baltimore, MD: Paul H. Brookes.

Maryland.gov 2017. *Definitions*, available at https://health.maryland.gov/odi/Pages/definitions.aspx (accessed July 27, 2017).

Ogbu, J.U. 1978. *Minority Education and Caste: The American System in Cross-Cultural Perspective.* San Diego, CA: Academic Press.

Ogbu, J.U. 1995. "Cultural Problems in Minority Education: Their Interpretations and Consequences—Part One: Theoretical Background." *The Urban Review* 27, no. 3, pp. 189–205.

Ogbu, J.U. 1996. "Ogbu's Theory." *Special Issues of Anthology and Education Quarterly* 27, no. 4.

Ouellet, J.F. 2007. "Consumer Racism and Its Effects on Domestic Cross-Ethnic Product Purchase: An Empirical Test in the United States, Canada, and France." *Journal of Marketing* 71, no. 1, pp. 113–28.

Oyez.org 1994. Available at https://oyez.org/cases/1994/93-1841 (accessed July 30, 2017).

Pages, E.R. 2005. "The Changing Demography of Entrepreneurship." *Local Economy* 20, no. 1, pp. 93–97.

Pbs.org 2017. Available at https://pbs.org/wnet/supremecourt/antebellum/landmark_dred.html (accessed July 30, 2017).

Peck, P. 2012. *Black Entrepreneurship on the Rise as Self-Employment Becomes an Option for Jobless Black Graduates.* Black Voices.

Porter, M.E., and M.R. Kramer. 2011. "Creating Shared Value." *Harvard Business Review* 89, nos. 1–2, 62–77, available at https://hbr.org/2011/01/the-big-idea-creating-shared-value (accessed July 30, 2017).

Pusey, M. 1963. *Charles Evans Hughes,* 2 vols. New York, NY: Columbia University Press.

Rachmawan, A., A.A. Lizar, and W.L.H. Mangundjaya. 2015. "The Role of Parent's Influence and Self-Efficacy On Entrepreneurial Intention." *The Journal of Developing Areas* 49, no. 3, pp. 417–30.

Reynolds, P. 2007. *Entrepreneurship in the United States: The Future is Now.* New York, NY: Springer.

Roberson, Q.M. 2006. "Disentangling the Meanings of Diversity and Inclusion in Organizations." *Group and Organization Management* 31, no. 2, pp. 212–36.

Rotter, J.B. 1942. "Level of Aspiration as a Method of Studying Personality. II. Development and Evaluation of a Controlled Method." *Journal of Experimental Psychology* 31, no. 5, 410–22, available at http://crossculturalleadership.yolasite.com/resources/The%20Social%20Learning%20

Rust College. 2017. *Quote of WEB Dubois,* available at http://rustcollege.edu/elam_chapel/September8.pdf (accessed September 15, 2017).

SBA 2017. Contracting, available at https://sba.gov/contracting/government-contracting-programs/what-small-business-set-aside (accessed December 20, 2017).

Shea, B. 2013. "Hiram Jackson's Goal: Update Real Times to Modern Times." *Crain's Detroit Business,* available at: http://crainsdetroit.com/article/20131013/NEWS/310139918/hiram-jacksons-goal-update-real-times-to-modern-times (accessed March 14, 2018).

Sherbin, L., and R. Rashid. 2017. "Diversity Does Not Stick Without Inclusion." *Harvard Business Review,* available at https://hbr.org/2017/02/diversity-doesnt-stick-without-inclusion (accessed July 25, 2017).

Splcenter.org 2017. *Fighting Hate,* available at https://splcenter.org/fighting-hate/intelligence-report/2003/radical-religio (accessed July 27, 2017).

Sullivan, D.M. 2007. "Minority Entrepreneurs: More Likely to Try, but Less Likely to Succeed." *Academy of Management Perspectives* 21, no. 1, pp. 78–79.

Tech News. 2012. Available at http://technews.tmcnet.com/news/2012/07/30/ 6473338.htm (accessed July 27, 2017).

The African American Lectionary. 2017. Available at http://theafricanamerican lectionary.org/PopupCulturalAid.asp?LRID=71 (accessed July 27, 2017).

USCCR.gov 2017. Available at http://usccr.gov/pubs/080505_fedprocadarand. pdf (accessed July 30, 2017).

Watkins, J.M. 2013. "Inquiry and Learning for Change." *Anthropology & Education Quarterly*, available at http://cae.americananthro.org/wp-content/ uploads/2013/03/Finn_Patrick-Literacy_with_an_Attitude.pdf (accessed July 30, 2017).

Zajonc, T. 2003. "Black Enterprise and the Legacy of Slavery." *Review of Black Political Economy* 30, no. 3, pp. 23–37.

CHAPTER 3

African American Entrepreneur Interviews

It is important that we share our experiences with other people. Your story will heal you, and your story will heal somebody else. When you tell your story, you free yourself and permit other people to acknowledge their own story.

—Iyanla Vanzant

In this section, the viewpoints of 21 African American entrepreneurs are offered. Specific names accompanying the interviews were omitted as a way of respecting personal privacy. The authors wish to express our thanks to the numerous respondents for generously sharing their time and their views.

The authors interviewed over a hundred African American entrepreneurs. Only 21 have been selected for follow-up conversations and analyzed in this book project. In the other cases, some questions were not answered. The authors decided to highlight and analyze only the interviews where the questions posed were all answered.

The insights gathered to constitute the views of the respondents and did not necessarily imply a shared viewpoint of the authors. The respondents were invited to reveal their honest and candid perceptions on the subject.

The featured interviews are current and real-life. These are not the views of researchers but actual voices of African American entrepreneurs.

The authors hope that the significant investment of time, energy, and resources to enhance the understanding of African American entrepreneurship will lead to a deeper knowledge of the subject. Moreover, we hope that these interviews will inspire others to follow the path of these successful role models.

Respondent 1

Interview

1. Here we ask you to provide us an overview of your family history. For example, was there an entrepreneur in your family? Did your family history influence your decision to start a business?

   My father started a business when I was a child, and I watched him nurture the business as I grew up. I desired to take over the family business as an adult and hopefully grow it into a much larger sustainable business.

2. What was your educational background? Do you have specific views on formal versus informal education? What are your views on African American entrepreneurial training programs? Has education contributed to your business success?

   I graduated with a bachelor's degree in Literature, Science and the Arts majoring in Radio and Television Production in 1974. I then entered The School of Communication and graduated with Master's degree in 1976 majoring in Broadcast Journalism.

3. Starting a new business is not something people take lightly. Why did you start yours? What steps did you take to start the business?

   Attended SBA workshops and enrolled in college and signed up for the military for the benefits of school and starting my own business and I received assistance from a minority small business center.

4. What challenges did you face when building your business, and how did you overcome them? Did you come across any unique circumstances because of your race?

   Requirements for minority businesses, that is, minority certification and access to invisible opportunities and lines of credit that do not exist.

5. What types of support were most helpful to you when you were building your business? For example, did your local community play a role in shaping your business interests and development, or maybe

it was a mentor? What or who was that one thing that made you believe, "Yes, I can do this!"

My family, the church, and friends.

6. What do you think are the essential skills needed for African American entrepreneurs, to succeed in America? Also, what personal attitudes do you think are essential?

Independence, the freedom to make decisions, and to do your own thing.

7. If you had the chance to start over again, would you do anything differently? More to the point, if you would, what's the reason?

Enjoy life while I was young.

8. How would you characterize the state of African American entrepreneurship in the United States? For instance, is it in the early stages, is it growing, or is it mature? Do you think it is open to all or limited to certain individuals? Is it viable from anywhere in the country, or more favorable in certain states?

It is still growing because the issues concerning minorities and their equal access to business opportunities are still being challenged.

9. Are you a member of any business organizations? Are these organizations unique to African Americans or open to all races? Did they contribute to your business success?

No.

10. Do you think social networks and personal connections are important to business? Did you use networking when building your business, and are your social networks race-based?

Yes.

11. If you could give advice to young African American entrepreneurs or other young people thinking about starting a business, what would be the most important thing, and why?

I would encourage anyone who wants to start a business to go to the free workshops offered by SBA and other community-based programs for minority business owners. Seek help to solve your problems and believe in yourself.

Respondent 2

Interview

1. Here we ask you to provide us an overview of your family history. For example, was there an entrepreneur in your family? Did your family history influence your decision to start a business?

   I saw combat service as a member of the Army reserves; I had done some landscaping before I was called to active duty to support myself while I attended college and to help out with the family business. I presume I could be described as a semi-entrepreneur because I sold my services as an independent contractor to my extended family, working every weekend and during breaks from school.

2. What was your educational background? Do you have specific views on formal versus informal education? What are your views on African American entrepreneurial training programs? Has education contributed to your business success?

   I only obtained an Associate degree, but I mingled with MBA students and was pushed by them regarding entrepreneurship. I completed my undergraduate degree, and I am currently enrolled in law school.

3. Starting a new business is not something people take lightly. Why did you start yours? What steps did you take to start the business?

   I attended business assistance program classes and took classes in entrepreneurship. I also participated in a mentoring program for African American males, funded by the state.

4. What challenges did you face when building your business, and how did you overcome them? Did you come across any unique circumstances as a result of your race?

Yes, the minority certification and qualification process and the assumption that I could find a majority partner for large-scale projects, banks willing to give financing for payroll and supplies.

5. What types of support were most helpful to you when you were building your business? For example, did your local community play a role in shaping your business interests and development, or maybe it was a mentor? What or who was that one thing that made you believe, "Yes, I can do this!"

The support came when my family and friends who started the business back in the 1950's expected to do business in the community shared stories about the importance of operating a business outside of the black community, along from local and national organizations.

6. What do you think are the essential skills needed for African American entrepreneurs, to succeed in America? Also, what personal attitudes do you think are essential?

I have lots of experience with clients and working with other agents on training them and getting them started with administrative assistance. I have the license and training in the industry.

7. If you had the chance to start over again, would you do anything differently? More to the point, if you would, what's the reason?

Go to school first and learn how to run a business and access to more mentors.

8. How would you characterize the state of African American entrepreneurship in the United States? For instance, is it in the early stages, is it growing, or is it mature? Do you think it is open to all or limited to certain individuals? Is it viable from anywhere in the country, or more favorable in certain states?

It is open to women minorities on a larger scale. African American men are still at the bottom of the pile.

9. Are you a member of any business organizations? Are these organizations unique to African Americans or open to all races? Did they contribute to your business success?

Yes, education, civic, and professional groups, for-profit, and arts organizations.

10. Do you think social networks and personal connections are important to business? Did you use networking when building your business, and are your social networks race-based?

No.

11. If you could advise young African American entrepreneurs or other young people thinking about starting a business, what would be the most important thing, and why?

Stay involved, do not rely on others for information.

Respondent 3

Interview

1. Here we ask you to provide us an overview of your family history. For example, was there an entrepreneur in your family? Did your family history influence your decision to start a business?

My father founded a construction company in the 1950s. My family's history is in the industry. I joined the family business.

2. What was your educational background? Do you have specific views on formal versus informal education? What are your views on African American entrepreneurial training programs? Has education contributed to your business success?

I have a BA in Business Management and Entrepreneurship. I believe in the old saying "when a child is dropped in the center of business they are like a ripple in the water eventually they travel with the current and become an entrepreneur."

3. Starting a new business is not something people take lightly. Why did you start yours? What steps did you take to start the business?

Find a banker and a mentor.

4. What challenges did you face when building your business, and how did you overcome them? Did you come across any unique circumstances as a result of your race?

Marketing was my challenge and teaching the workforce the business and the linkage to political agendas and economic sustainability in the African American urban communities.

5. What types of support were most helpful to you when you were building your business? For example, did your local community play a role in shaping your business interests and development, or maybe it was a mentor? What or who was that one thing that made you believe, "Yes, I can do this!"

Working with the unions, local trade organizations, and majority firms.

6. What do you think are the essential skills needed for African American entrepreneurs, to succeed in America? Also, what personal attitudes do you think are essential?

Communication.

7. If you had the chance to start over again, would you do anything differently? More to the point, if you would, what's the reason?

I would find a mentor.

8. How would you characterize the state of African American entrepreneurship in the United States? For instance, is it in the early stages, is it growing, or is it mature? Do you think it is open to all or limited to certain individuals? Is it viable from anywhere in the country, or more favorable in certain states?

Minority set-aside rulings have been upheld so this state is working in favor of minority business owners.

9. Are you a member of any business organizations? Are these organizations unique to African Americans or open to all races? Did they contribute to your business success?

   Yes, the actors' guild and other organizations related to my industry.

10. Do you think social networks and personal connections are important to business? Did you use networking when building your business, and are your social networks race-based?

   Yes, my networks are international, my business is global communication is important.

11. If you could advise young African American entrepreneurs or other young people thinking about starting a business, what would be the most important thing, and why?

   The women who I read about and the things I read about and pictures of African American women in the theater. I wrote plays about these women and learned about them.

Respondent 4

Interview

1. Here we ask you to provide us an overview of your family history. For example, was there an entrepreneur in your family? Did your family history influence your decision to start a business?

   We are a family owned business. My husband and I have run the business for three years, and it is an uphill battle, but it is going well.

2. What was your educational background? Do you have specific views on formal versus informal education? What are your views on African American entrepreneurial training programs? Has education contributed to your business success?

   I dropped out of college to pursue my desire to own a restaurant.

3. Starting a new business isn't something people take lightly. Why did you start yours? What steps did you take to start the business?

I watched my father run his business.

4. What challenges did you face when building your business, and how did you overcome them? Did you come across any unique circumstances as a result of your race?

The changes in the regulations, the requirements for minority companies.

5. What types of support were most helpful to you when you were building your business? For example, did your local community play a role in shaping your business interests and development, or maybe it was a mentor? What or who was that one thing that made you believe, "Yes, I can do this!"

Awards received from national and local organizations, active participation in my church, and community advocacy.

6. What do you think are the essential skills needed for African American entrepreneurs, to succeed in America? Also, what personal attitudes do you think are essential?

Looking back, Broadway needs more things such as singing and dancing, short plays are available, but I cannot make that comparison, for the African American the subsidy to support the artist and opportunities is important, to the black theater to still be active and attract young play writers and actors.

7. If you had the chance to start over again, would you do anything differently? More to the point, if you would, what is the reason?

Pay more attention and learn from my father and others in my community how to run the business.

8. How would you characterize the state of African American entrepreneurship in the United States. For instance, is it in the early stages, is

it growing, or is it mature? Do you think it is open to all or limited to certain individuals? Is it viable from anywhere in the country, or more favorable in certain states?

We are a family owned business with 35 years' experience, and our reputation is our strength, our weaknesses are time management and succession planning. We are a referral service, and we have not brand-imaged the company with the succeeding generations' ability to provide services based on the tradition of excellence practiced by original owners, our father.

9. Are you a member of any business organizations? Are these organizations unique to African Americans or open to all races? Did they contribute to your business success?

Yes, professional, and African American fraternal organizations.

10. Do you think social networks and personal connections are important to business? Did you use networking when building your business, and are your social networks race-based?

Yes.

11. If you could advise young African American entrepreneurs or other young people thinking about starting a business, what would be the most important thing, and why?

Learn as much as you can before you start.

Respondent 5

Interview

1. Here we ask you to provide us an overview of your family history. For example, was there an entrepreneur in your family? Did your family history influence your decision to start a business?

My mother was a union member, and the classes offered by her union allowed me to learn how to be an actor. I began acting like a child and stayed in business.

2. What was your educational background? Do you have specific views on formal versus informal education? What are your views on African American entrepreneurial training programs? Has education contributed to your business success?

   My formal education taught me the consequences of my actions and my informal education taught me when to take a risk without consequence.

3. Starting a new business isn't something people take lightly. Why did you start yours? What steps did you take to start the business?

   I worked in the family business since I was little.

4. What challenges did you face when building your business, and how did you overcome them? Did you come across any unique circumstances as a result of your race?

   Overcoming my sense of powerlessness when doing business with white people or people outside my neighborhood.

5. What types of support were most helpful to you when you were building your business? For example, did your local community play a role in shaping your business interests and development, or maybe it was a mentor? What or who was that one thing that made you believe, "Yes, I can do this!"

   I needed information and access to the major corporation I wanted to pair.

6. What do you think are the essential skills needed for African American entrepreneurs, to succeed in America? Also, what personal attitudes do you think are essential?

   Learning the requirements for getting business if you want to be listed as a minority business.

7. If you had the chance to start over again, would you do anything differently? More to the point, if you would, what is the reason?

   Education. There was too much I just did not know.

8. How would you characterize the state of African American entrepreneurship in the United States? For instance, is it in the early stages, is it growing, or is it mature? Do you think it is open to all or limited to certain individuals? Is it viable from anywhere in the country, or more favorable in certain states?

Open to all if they want to work hard, learn the requirements, and work with others.

9. Are you a member of any business organizations? Are these organizations unique to African Americans or open to all races? Did they contribute to your business success?

Various community organizations supporting the arts contribute to not only the actor but also the community.

10. Do you think social networks and personal connections are important to business? Did you use networking when building your business, and are your social networks race-based?

No, too social, too expensive.

11. If you could advise young African American entrepreneurs or other young people thinking about starting a business, what would be the most important thing, and why?

Stay in school.

Respondent 6

Interview

1. Here we ask you to provide us an overview of your family history. For example, was there an entrepreneur in your family? Did your family history influence your decision to start a business?

Yes, my family and my husband's family owned farms.

2. What was your educational background? Do you have specific views on formal versus informal education? What are your views on

African American entrepreneurial training programs? Has education contributed to your business success?

I am a graduate of a state university undergraduate program and Law School.

3. Starting a new business is not something people take lightly. Why did you start yours? What steps did you take to start the business?

   I worked in the corporate world for many years. Inclusion was a mandate, upper mobility into management was not. I left the corporation and started my business.

4. What challenges did you face when building your business, and how did you overcome them? Did you come across any unique circumstances as a result of your race?

   I own a cleaning franchise, and they trained me and continued to provide classes on the latest ways to clean commercially and for private homes.

5. What types of support were most helpful to you when you were building your business? For example, did your local community play a role in shaping your business interests and development, or maybe it was a mentor? What or who was that one thing that made you believe, "Yes, I can do this!"

   The business evaluations by the franchise and my customers.

6. What do you think are the essential skills needed for African American entrepreneurs, to succeed in America? Also, what personal attitudes do you think are essential?

   Becoming certified as a minority business because the program enhanced access to some of the services my business needs. It is a valuable experience. I have been exposed to much useful information. I also met a lot of interesting people. They have helped me with financial planning, insurance terms, and a lot of general business things that is has been an incredible experience.

7. If you had the chance to start over again, would you do anything differently? More to the point, if you would, what's the reason?

Keep notes on the little business tips my mother gave me over the years.

8. How would you characterize the state of African American entrepreneurship in the United States? For instance, is it in the early stages, is it growing, or is it mature? Do you think it is open to all or limited to certain individuals? Is it viable from anywhere in the country, or more favorable in certain states?

It's growing in acceptance. Women studies, my programs, and roles about females and the similarity about women created an opportunity for acting and writing off-Broadway.

9. Are you a member of any business organizations? Are these organizations unique to African Americans or open to all races? Did they contribute to your business success?

No, but I learned a lot from the classes they provided.

10. Do you think social networks and personal connections are important to business? Did you use networking when building your business, and are your social networks race-based?

Yes, the owner of a telecommunications company who works with me during the growth phase, the most pressing need is to help me establish contacts and getting to people within the corporation that recognize the value, because if they do not acknowledge the value. He is mentoring my business and acts as a business coach. He authored a book.

11. If you could advise young African American entrepreneurs or other young people thinking about starting a business, what would be the most important thing, and why?

Follow your heart and your passion.

Respondent 7

Interview

1. Here we ask you to provide us an overview of your family history. For example, was there an entrepreneur in your family? Did your family history influence your decision to start a business?

   No, my job in the factory ended, and I had to contribute to the support of my family. My family had a history of self-employment in the service industry. They did not register their business. I decided to start a business. They influence my decision to register my business and network outside of the community and the church.

2. What was your educational background? Do you have specific views on formal versus informal education? What are your views on African American entrepreneurial training programs? Has education contributed to your business success?

   Some college, certification courses for the industry, workshops on how to run a business, friends and older business owner mentors, they all contributed.

3. Starting a new business isn't something people take lightly. Why did you start yours? What steps did you take to start the business?

   I took classes online to obtain certain skills and knowledge. I hired an accountant and attorney.

4. What challenges did you face when building your business, and how did you overcome them? Did you come across any unique circumstances as a result of your race?

   Race. I have been in business for three years, and it is an uphill battle. Our weaknesses are that we are a little too sweet when people in the community when they do not want to pay for the services because they do not have the money. Sometimes people take kindness for weakness.

5. What types of support were most helpful to you when you were building your business? For example, did your local community play a role in shaping your business interests and development, or maybe it was a mentor? What or who was that one thing that made you believe, "Yes, I can do this!"

My family and friends, and associates from my previous corporate job.

6. What do you think are the essential skills needed for African American entrepreneurs, to succeed in America? Also, what personal attitudes do you think are essential?

To know what I don't know and seek right help.

7. If you had the chance to start over again, would you do anything differently? More to the point, if you would, what's the reason?

Obtain a degree in my field of interest.

8. How would you characterize the state of African American entrepreneurship in the United States? For instance, is it in the early stages, is it growing, or is it mature? Do you think it is open to all or limited to certain individuals? Is it viable from anywhere in the country, or more favorable in certain states?

Complicated.

9. Are you a member of any business organizations? Are these organizations unique to African Americans or open to all races? Did they contribute to your business success?

Yes, mainstream American business organizations, active participation in political fundraisers, and others in the African American community.

10. Do you think social networks and personal connections are important to business? Did you use networking when building your business, and are your social networks race-based?

Yes, if selective about which groups offer valuable networking and which are just social, drinking get-togethers.

11. If you could advise young African American entrepreneurs or other young people thinking about starting a business, what would be the most important thing, and why?

Find a mentor, participate in minority small business advocates and political events.

Respondent 8

Interview

1. Here we ask you to provide us an overview of your family history. For example, was there an entrepreneur in your family? Did your family history influence your decision to start a business?

Yes, my Father in the Catholic Church informal network of business owners, regardless of race or gender.

2. What was your educational background? Do you have specific views on formal versus informal education? What are your views on African American entrepreneurial training programs? Has education contributed to your business success?

As an ex-offender, it was not easy. I had to find classes and workshops that accepted people with a criminal record.

3. Starting a new business isn't something people take lightly. Why did you start yours? What steps did you take to start the business?

African American construction trade business owner gave me free trade manuals to learn from allowed me to follow him around his shop and gave me the first opportunity to work in the trades on one of his construction projects.

4. What challenges did you face when building your business, and how did you overcome them? Did you come across any unique circumstances as a result of your race?

Our business is located in an urban city, and we are a sole proprietor in the early stages of business, and I will primarily receive debt finance through a local bank investor of private small business association. We forecasted 60 percent debt, and the rest will be invested back into the company. We carry hard to find items for sporting apparel, so you think of our brand name.

5. What types of support were most helpful to you when you were building your business? For example, did your local community play a role in shaping your business interests and development, or maybe it was a mentor? What or who was that one thing that made you believe, "Yes, I can do this!"

   Having failed before on the job and in the community, I was confident I would not fail again. I was also committed to not committing a crime again. Nineteen years in prison taught me not ever to do anything that would put me back in jail.

6. What do you think are the essential skills needed for African American entrepreneurs, to succeed in America? Also, what personal attitudes do you think are essential?

   Networking skills, finding, and trusting assistance from people not a part of my family or friends from my other life.

7. If you had the chance to start over again, would you do anything differently? More to the point, if you would, what's the reason?

   I would have stayed in college, graduated, and not get involved in the street.

8. How would you characterize the state of African American entrepreneurship in the United States? For instance, is it in the early stages, is it growing, or is it mature? Do you think it is open to all or limited to certain individuals? Is it viable from anywhere in the country, or more favorable in certain states?

   I do not know about other countries; I only wonder if you work hard you have a better chance at success.

9. Are you a member of any business organizations? Are these organizations unique to African Americans or open to all races? Did they contribute to your business success?

Yes, the black trades council network.

10. Do you think social networks and personal connections are important to business? Did you use networking when building your business, and are your social networks race-based?

No, too often the social outweighs the business portion.

11. If you could advise young African American entrepreneurs or other young people thinking about starting a business, what would be the most important thing, and why?

Pay attention to those in business and learn from them.

Respondent 9

Interview

1. Here we ask you to provide us an overview of your family history. For example, was there an entrepreneur in your family? Did your family history influence your decision to start a business?

My family was the owner of a master franchise they developed from the ground-up.

2. What was your educational background? Do you have specific views on formal versus informal education? What are your views on African American entrepreneurial training programs? Has education contributed to your business success?

Yes, a college education is critical to success in a global world.

3. Starting a new business isn't something people take lightly. Why did you start yours? What steps did you take to start the business?

I majored in business in college.

4. What challenges did you face when building your business, and how did you overcome them? Did you come across any unique circumstances as a result of your race?

I have been doing video productions for PBS station for 20 years, and this was very valuable, I started my business three years ago. I have a well-rounded technical background, but not significant business knows how. I can come up with different marketing strategies to reach out to marketing to different markets to find various applications for production in various industries. I need to return to school or attend workshops. I need to understand bookkeeping and the necessary backbone to what it takes to run a business definitively say it has been an experience even to this point.

5. What types of support were most helpful to you when you were building your business? For example, did your local community play a role in shaping your business interests and development, or maybe it was a mentor? What or who was that one thing that made you believe, "Yes, I can do this!"

My father kept pushing.

6. What do you think are the essential skills needed for African American entrepreneurs, to succeed in America? Also, what personal attitudes do you think are essential?

Ability to take what I learned to my business.

7. If you had the chance to start over again, would you do anything differently? More to the point, if you would, what's the reason?

Done more research to develop a strategic and marketing plan.

8. How would you characterize the state of African American entrepreneurship in the United States? For instance, is it in the early stages, is it growing, or is it mature? Do you think it is open to all or limited to certain individuals? Is it viable from anywhere in the country, or more favorable in certain states?

Start-up stages are difficult, because of limited opportunities available to people like me. Big cities offer more, such as Atlanta, the District, New York, City, LA, Cleveland, and Detroit.

9. Are you a member of any business organizations? Are these organizations unique to African Americans or open to all races? Did they contribute to your business success?

   Yes, organizations that offer business assistance programs for minorities.

10. Do you think social networks and personal connections are important to business? Did you use networking when building your business, and are your social networks race-based?

    Yes, any opportunity to meet and learn from new people is rewarding.

11. If you could advise young African American entrepreneurs or other young people thinking about starting a business, what would be the most important thing, and why?

    Soak up as much knowledge as possible from others, but follow your path.

Respondent 10

Interview

1. Here we ask you to provide us an overview of your family history. For example, was there an entrepreneur in your family? Did your family history influence your decision to start a business?

   Yes.

2. What was your educational background? Do you have specific views on formal versus informal education? What are your views on African American entrepreneurial training programs? Has education contributed to your business success?

   Yes, that is how I can multi-tasking as an author, producer, and actor.

3. Starting a new business isn't something people take lightly. Why did you start yours? What steps did you take to start the business?

   I used networking opportunities to meet people who could help me start a business.

4. What challenges did you face when building your business, and how did you overcome them? Did you come across any unique circumstances as a result of your race?

   Access to capital.

5. What types of support were most helpful to you when you were building your business? For example, did your local community play a role in shaping your business interests and development, or maybe it was a mentor? What or who was that one thing that made you believe, "Yes, I can do this!"

   Initial success was more than expected.

6. What do you think are the essential skills needed for African American entrepreneurs, to succeed in America? Also, what personal attitudes do you think are essential?

   Understanding the regulatory pitfalls facing a new business.

7. If you had the chance to start over again, would you do anything differently? More to the point, if you would, what's the reason?

   Listen more carefully to those who had vast amounts of business and were willing to share with me.

8. How would you characterize the state of African American entrepreneurship in the United States? For instance, is it in the early stages, is it growing, or is it mature? Do you think it is open to all or limited to certain individuals? Is it viable from anywhere in the country, or more favorable in certain states?

   Opportunities are available, but gaining access to them is challenging.

9. Are you a member of any business organizations? Are these organizations unique to African Americans or open to all races? Did they contribute to your business success?

Networking organizations that are open to all.

10. Do you think social networks and personal connections are important to business? Did you use networking when building your business, and are your social networks race-based?

Except for golf, social activities can be distracting.

11. If you could advise young African American entrepreneurs or other young people thinking about starting a business, what would be the most important thing, and why?

Know what you do not know.

Respondent 11

Interview

1. Here we ask you to provide us an overview of your family history. For example, was there an entrepreneur in your family? Did your family history influence your decision to start a business?

My grandparents and siblings were entrepreneurs.

2. What was your educational background? Do you have specific views on formal versus informal education? What are your views on African American entrepreneurial training programs? Has education contributed to your business success?

My husband and I finished high school and took business courses at night, I returned to school, and I have a business management degree.

3. Starting a new business is not something people take lightly. Why did you start yours? What steps did you take to start the business?

Business assistance programs.

4. What challenges did you face when building your business, and how did you overcome them? Did you come across any unique circumstances as a result of your race?

Finding the right people to help the business grow.

5. What types of support were most helpful to you when you were building your business? For example, did your local community play a role in shaping your business interests and development, or maybe it was a mentor? What or who was that one thing that made you believe, "Yes, I can do this!"

Acceptance by my peers and competitors.

6. What do you think are the essential skills needed for African American entrepreneurs, to succeed in America? Also, what personal attitudes do you think are essential?

Certification process.

7. If you had the chance to start over again, would you do anything differently? More to the point, if you would, what's the reason?

Enroll in business assistance programs.

8. How would you characterize the state of African American entrepreneurship in the United States? For instance, is it in the early stages, is it growing, or is it mature? Do you think it is open to all or limited to certain individuals? Is it viable from anywhere in the country, or more favorable in certain states?

Federal, state, and local governments are both supportive of minority business, while at the same time creating roadblocks to success.

9. Are you a member of any business organizations? Are these organizations unique to African Americans or open to all races? Did they contribute to your business success?

Mentoring organizations that are open to all.

10. Do you think social networks and personal connections are important to business? Did you use networking when building your business, and are your social networks race-based?

Social and networking events and organizations are a hit or miss proposition.

11. If you could advise young African American entrepreneurs or other young people thinking about starting a business, what would be the most important thing, and why?

Ask questions. There are no dumb questions.

Respondent 12

Interview

1. Here we ask you to provide us an overview of your family history. For example, was there an entrepreneur in your family? Did your family history influence your decision to start a business?

Yes, my family members owned a video production studio.

2. What was your educational background? Do you have specific views on formal versus informal education? What are your views on African American entrepreneurial training programs? Has education contributed to your business success?

No formal education, school of hard knocks.

3. Starting a new business is not something people take lightly. Why did you start yours? What steps did you take to start the business?

I needed the money for my family, and they supported me in my endeavor.

4. What challenges did you face when building your business, and how did you overcome them? Did you come across any unique circumstances because of your race?

Expanding outside my minority community.

5. What types of support were most helpful to you when you were building your business? For example, did your local community play a role in shaping your business interests and development, or maybe it was a mentor? What or who was that one thing that made you believe, "Yes, I can do this!"

The family has my back.

6. What do you think are the essential skills needed for African American entrepreneurs, to succeed in America? Also, what personal attitudes do you think are essential?

Ability to evaluate my employees to utilize their skill set better.

7. If you had the chance to start over again, would you do anything differently? More to the point, if you would, what's the reason?

Education.

8. How would you characterize the state of African American entrepreneurship in the United States? For instance, is it in the early stages, is it growing, or is it mature? Do you think it is open to all or limited to certain individuals? Is it viable from anywhere in the country, or more favorable in certain states?

Minority businesses no longer have defined markets, which makes competing with majority companies much more challenging.

9. Are you a member of any business organizations? Are these organizations unique to African Americans or open to all races? Did they contribute to your business success?

Not a member of any organization. Rely on family and friends.

10. Do you think social networks and personal connections are important to business? Did you use networking when building your business, and are your social networks race-based?

No, too much socialization.

11. If you could advise young African American entrepreneurs or other young people thinking about starting a business, what would be the most important thing, and why?

Attend as many classes as possible to understand the challenges that you face.

Respondent 13

Interview

1. Here we ask you to provide us an overview of your family history. For example, was there an entrepreneur in your family? Did your family history influence your decision to start a business?

My parents spent years talking about starting a business and never did one thing to make it happen; when my opportunity came, I was determined to try to succeed.

2. What was your educational background? Do you have specific views on formal versus informal education? What are your views on African American entrepreneurial training programs? Has education contributed to your business success?

Some business training programs and seminars, and the assistance I received when I came home.

3. Starting a new business is not something people take lightly. Why did you start yours? What steps did you take to start the business?

SBA business start-up programs.

4. What challenges did you face when building your business, and how did you overcome them? Did you come across any unique circumstances as a result of your race?

I need private investors willing to work with me for the long haul.

5. What types of support were most helpful to you when you were building your business? For example, did your local community play a role in shaping your business interests and development, or maybe it was a mentor? What or who was that one thing that made you believe, "Yes, I can do this!"

I gained access to capital.

6. What do you think are the essential skills needed for African American entrepreneurs, to succeed in America? Also, what personal attitudes do you think are essential?

Understanding financial terms and conditions to be able to assess profit and loss scenarios.

7. If you had the chance to start over again, would you do anything differently? More to the point, if you would, what's the reason?

Plan to ensure I had the resources to start a business properly.

8. How would you characterize the state of African American entrepreneurship in the United States? For instance, is it in the early stages, is it growing, or is it mature? Do you think it is open to all or limited to certain individuals? Is it viable from anywhere in the country, or more favorable in certain states?

We still lack access to adequate capital.

9. Are you a member of any business organizations? Are these organizations unique to African Americans or open to all races? Did they contribute to your business success?

Yes, various organizations in my field of interest offer assistance, mentors, classes, and places to discuss ideas.

10. Do you think social networks and personal connections are important to business? Did you use networking when building your business, and are your social networks race-based?

Yes, networking helps.

11. If you could advise young African American entrepreneurs or other young people thinking about starting a business, what would be the most important thing, and why?

Education is the key.

Respondent 14

Interview

1. Here we ask you to provide us an overview of your family history. For example, was there an entrepreneur in your family? Did your family history influence your decision to start a business?

    My father owned a bar, and I watched him work from the time I was little. Business was bred into me.

2. What was your educational background? Do you have specific views on formal versus informal education? What are your views on African American entrepreneurial training programs? Has education contributed to your business success?

    No formal education, but I watched my family run a small business.

3. Starting a new business is not something people take lightly. Why did you start yours? What steps did you take to start the business?

    Wanted to be my own boss.

4. What challenges did you face when building your business, and how did you overcome them? Did you come across any unique circumstances as a result of your race?

    Access to capital, and workforce.

5. What types of support were most helpful to you when you were building your business? For example, did your local community play a role in shaping your business interests and development, or maybe it was a mentor? What or who was that one thing that made you believe, "Yes, I can do this!"

    I had a great mentor.

6. What do you think are the essential skills needed for African American entrepreneurs, to succeed in America? Also, what personal attitudes do you think are essential?

Networking.

7. If you had the chance to start over again, would you do anything differently? More to the point, if you would, what's the reason?

Utilize family and friends with the knowledge I needed such as accountants, lawyers, marketers/salesperson, andand so on.

8. How would you characterize the state of African American entrepreneurship in the United States? For instance, is it in the early stages, is it growing, or is it mature? Do you think it is open to all or limited to certain individuals? Is it viable from anywhere in the country, or more favorable in certain states?

African American entrepreneurship was easier and fast growing in the past when we sold to, bought from, and supported each other. It feels like that is no longer true in America.

9. Are you a member of any business organizations? Are these organizations unique to African Americans or open to all races? Did they contribute to your business success?

Yes, networking organizations.

10. Do you think social networks and personal connections are important to business? Did you use networking when building your business, and are your social networks race-based?

Groups such as Rotary, open to all, can be of great assistance.

11. If you could advise young African American entrepreneurs or other young people thinking about starting a business, what would be the most important thing, and why?

Believe in yourself.

Respondent 15

Interview

1. Here we ask you to provide us an overview of your family history. For example, was there an entrepreneur in your family? Did your family history influence your decision to start a business?

   My mother worked day and night to make a go of her business and barely held on too. I was aware of the pitfalls and challenges when I decided to start a business.

2. What was your educational background? Do you have specific views on formal versus informal education? What are your views on African American entrepreneurial training programs? Has education contributed to your business success?

   My training helped, but work experience was the best teacher.

3. Starting a new business is not something people take lightly. Why did you start yours? What steps did you take to start the business?

   The opportunity arose, and I was in the right place at the right time.

4. What challenges did you face when building your business, and how did you overcome them? Did you come across any unique circumstances as a result of your race?

   I need mentors to help in the areas I am unfamiliar.

5. What types of support were most helpful to you when you were building your business? For example, did your local community play a role in shaping your business interests and development, or maybe it was a mentor? What or who was that one thing that made you believe, "Yes, I can do this!"

   Real-life experience combined to keep me in the game.

6. What do you think are the essential skills needed for African American entrepreneurs, to succeed in America? Also, what personal attitudes do you think are essential?

HR requirements.

7. If you had the chance to start over again, would you do anything differently? More to the point, if you would, what's the reason?

Be open to advice from everyone. I was too afraid to share my ideas for fear they would be stolen.

8. How would you characterize the state of African American entrepreneurship in the United States? For instance, is it in the early stages, is it growing, or is it mature? Do you think it is open to all or limited to certain individuals? Is it viable from anywhere in the country, or more favorable in certain states?

Opportunities abound. However, for everyone that is successful, too many fail for lack of resources.

9. Are you a member of any business organizations? Are these organizations unique to African Americans or open to all races? Did they contribute to your business success?

Business assistance organizations open to all.

10. Do you think social networks and personal connections are important to business? Did you use networking when building your business, and are your social networks race-based?

Membership in alumni organizations.

11. If you could advise young African American entrepreneurs or other young people thinking about starting a business, what would be the most important thing, and why?

Be willing to share to grow.

Respondent 16

Interview

1. Here we ask you to provide us an overview of your family history. For example, was there an entrepreneur in your family? Did your family history influence your decision to start a business?

   While my parents never owned a business, they worked for entrepreneurs all their lives and instilled in me a desire to be my own boss.

2. What was your educational background? Do you have specific views on formal versus informal education? What are your views on African American entrepreneurial training programs? Has education contributed to your business success?

   College degree.

3. Starting a new business is not something people take lightly. Why did you start yours? What steps did you take to start the business?

   Prison taught me quite a bit about business.

4. What challenges did you face when building your business, and how did you overcome them? Did you come across any unique circumstances as a result of your race?

   Marketing and capital.

5. What types of support were most helpful to you when you were building your business? For example, did your local community play a role in shaping your business interests and development, or maybe it was a mentor? What or who was that one thing that made you believe, "Yes, I can do this!"

   My teachers and friends kept encouraging me even when things looked bleak.

6. What do you think are the essential skills needed for African American entrepreneurs, to succeed in America? Also, what personal attitudes do you think are essential?

Knowing how to find and use mentors.

7. If you had the chance to start over again, would you do anything differently? More to the point, if you would, what is the reason?

Be willing to share the business with others ready to invest in my ideas. Too many times I refused to part with any percentage, so I kept 100 percent of a small unsustainable business rather than 60 percent of a much larger successful enterprise.

8. How would you characterize the state of African American entrepreneurship in the United States? For instance, is it in the early stages, is it growing, or is it mature? Do you think it is open to all or limited to certain individuals? Is it viable from anywhere in the country, or more favorable in certain states?

Government programs continue to assist minority businesses.

9. Are you a member of any business organizations? Are these organizations unique to African Americans or open to all races? Did they contribute to your business success?

No.

10. Do you think social networks and personal connections are important to business? Did you use networking when building your business, and are your social networks race-based?

Yes and No. I have found some very helpful and others no help at all.

11. If you could advise young African American entrepreneurs or other young people thinking about starting a business, what would be the most important thing, and why?

Utilize all tools available to assist you, business assistance programs, government grants, law, and regulations, and so on.

Respondent 17

Interview

1. Here we ask you to provide us an overview of your family history. For example, was there an entrepreneur in your family? Did your family history influence your decision to start a business?

   No, but family and people kept coming to me to buy my goods.

2. What was your educational background? Do you have specific views on formal versus informal education? What are your views on African American entrepreneurial training programs? Has education contributed to your business success?

   We are a sports apparel equipment company for recreational facilities, trophies for organizations and youth.

3. Starting a new business is not something people take lightly. Why did you start yours? What steps did you take to start the business?

   State programs for start-ups.

4. What challenges did you face when building your business, and how did you overcome them? Did you come across any unique circumstances as a result of your race?

   Key personnel, bookkeepers, secretary, and so on, were helpful.

5. What types of support were most useful to you when you were building your business? For example, did your local community play a role in shaping your business interests and development, or maybe it was a mentor? What or who was that one thing that made you believe, "Yes, I can do this!"

   My mother believed in me even if I did have doubts myself.

6. What do you think are the essential skills needed for African American entrepreneurs, to succeed in America? Also, what personal attitudes do you think are essential?

   How to find business assistance programs that will help my unique business.

7. If you had the chance to start over again, would you do anything differently? More to the point, if you would, what's the reason?

   Utilize the laws, regulations, and programs available to assist my business.

8. How would you characterize the state of African American entrepreneurship in the United States? For instance, is it in the early stages, is it growing, or is it mature? Do you think it is open to all or limited to certain individuals? Is it viable from anywhere in the country, or more favorable in certain states?

   The number of African Americans will become entrepreneurs appears to be shrinking. The challenges today are daunting.

9. Are you a member of any business organizations? Are these organizations unique to African Americans or open to all races? Did they contribute to your business success?

   Yes, my golf group offers access to many business leaders and mentors.

10. Do you think social networks and personal connections are important to business? Did you use networking when building your business, and are your social networks race-based?

    Yes.

11. If you could advise young African American entrepreneurs or other young people thinking about starting a business, what would be the most important thing, and why?

    Do not let failure define you. I know a successful entrepreneur may have failed many times before he succeeded.

Respondent 18

Interview

1. Here we ask you to provide us an overview of your family history. For example, was there an entrepreneur in your family? Did your family history influence your decision to start a business?

My brother started his own companies, and this gave me the courage to try my hand at owning a business.

2. What was your educational background? Do you have specific views on formal versus informal education? What are your views on African American entrepreneurial training programs? Has education contributed to your business success?

Online MBA degree.

3. Starting a new business is not something people take lightly. Why did you start yours? What steps did you take to start the business?

Family persuasion.

4. What challenges did you face when building your business, and how did you overcome them? Did you come across any unique circumstances as a result of your race?

Investors.

5. What types of support were most helpful to you when you were building your business? For example, did your local community play a role in shaping your business interests and development, or maybe it was a mentor? What or who was that one thing that made you believe, "Yes, I can do this!"

The military.

6. What do you think are the essential skills needed for African American entrepreneurs, to succeed in America? Also, what personal attitudes do you think are essential?

Separating family and friends from business decisions.

7. If you had the chance to start over again, would you do anything differently? More to the point, if you would, what's the reason?

Obtain a college education majoring in business.

8. How would you characterize the state of African American entrepreneurship in the United States? For instance, is it in the early stages, is it growing, or is it mature? Do you think it is open to all or limited to certain individuals? Is it viable from anywhere in the country, or more favorable in certain states?

The African American business is alive and well.

9. Are you a member of any business organizations? Are these organizations unique to African Americans or open to all races? Did they contribute to your business success?

Yes, alumni organizations.

10. Do you think social networks and personal connections are important to business? Did you use networking when building your business, and are your social networks race-based?

Maybe.

11. If you could advise young African American entrepreneurs or other young people thinking about starting a business, what would be the most important thing, and why?

Ask questions and listen.

Respondent 19

Interview

1. Here we ask you to provide us an overview of your family history. For example, was there an entrepreneur in your family? Did your family history influence your decision to start a business?

I had no relatives in the business. Neither did any encourage me to go into business.

2. What was your educational background? Do you have specific views on formal versus informal education? What are your views on

African American entrepreneurial training programs? Has education contributed to your business success?

No formal education.

3. Starting a new business is not something people take lightly. Why did you start yours? What steps did you take to start the business?

College courses got me started as an exercise, and I kept the business going.

4. What challenges did you face when building your business, and how did you overcome them? Did you come across any unique circumstances because of your race?

Capital that is not debt only.

5. What types of support were most helpful to you when you were building your business? For example, did your local community play a role in shaping your business interests and development, or it was a mentor? What or who was that one thing that made you believe, "Yes, I can do this!"

Anything was possible is something I learned in church and from my coach in high school.

6. What do you think are the essential skills needed for African American entrepreneurs, to succeed in America? Also, what personal attitudes do you think are essential?

Finance.

7. If you had the chance to start over again, would you do anything differently? More to the point, if you would, what's the reason?

Find and keep mentors, someone to help you without charging for their help.

8. How would you characterize the state of African American entrepreneurship in the United States? For instance, is it in the early stages, is

it growing, or is it mature? Do you think it is open to all or limited to certain individuals? Is it viable from anywhere in the country, or more favorable in certain states?

While there are many African American businesses in this country, they stay small and have difficulty growing to the next level of success.

9. Are you a member of any business organizations? Are these organizations unique to African Americans or open to all races? Did they contribute to your business success?

No, just family.

10. Do you think social networks and personal connections are important to business? Did you use networking when building your business, and are your social networks race-based?

Very useful to find mentors.

11. If you could advise young African American entrepreneurs or other young people thinking about starting a business, what would be the most important thing, and why?

Find a good mentor.

Respondent 20

Interview

1. Here we ask you to provide us an overview of your family history. For example, was there an entrepreneur in your family? Did your family history influence your decision to start a business?

My aunt did hair in the basement of her house, and she would explain to me the difficulties of business.

2. What was your educational background? Do you have specific views on formal versus informal education? What are your views on African American entrepreneurial training programs? Has education contributed to your business success?

No, I learned from my family and work.

3. Starting a new business is not something people take lightly. Why did you start yours? What steps did you take to start the business?

Business assistance programs.

4. What challenges did you face when building your business, and how did you overcome them? Did you come across any unique circumstances as a result of your race?

Mentors.

5. What types of support were most helpful to you when you were building your business? For example, did your local community play a role in shaping your business interests and development, or maybe it was a mentor? What or who was that one thing that made you believe, "Yes, I can do this!"

Instructors at the Business Assistance Program stayed with me.

6. What do you think are the essential skills needed for African American entrepreneurs, to succeed in America? Also, what personal attitudes do you think are essential?

Regulations.

7. If you had the chance to start over again, would you do anything differently? More to the point, if you would, what's the reason?

Put earnings back into the business.

8. How would you characterize the state of African American entrepreneurship in the United States? For instance, is it in the early stages, is it growing, or is it mature? Do you think it is open to all or limited to certain individuals? Is it viable from anywhere in the country, or more favorable in certain states?

African American entrepreneurs fear that they are losing the support of the government as other minority groups outpace them.

9. Are you a member of any business organizations? Are these organizations unique to African Americans or open to all races? Did they contribute to your business success?

Yes, bar association programs open to all.

10. Do you think social networks and personal connections are important to business? Did you use networking when building your business, and are your social networks race-based?

No.

11. If you could advise young African American entrepreneurs or other young people thinking about starting a business, what would be the most important thing, and why?

Enjoy what you are doing.

Respondent 21

Interview

1. Here we ask you to provide us an overview of your family history. For example, was there an entrepreneur in your family? Did your family history influence your decision to start a business?

No family members, only friends who enticed me to pursue a business venture.

2. What was your educational background? Do you have specific views on formal versus informal education? What are your views on African American entrepreneurial training programs? Has education contributed to your business success?

No, my father trained me how to mix the pest control when I was in high school. My education did not help.

3. Starting a new business is not something people take lightly. Why did you start yours? What steps did you take to start the business?

Family and friends' encouragement. My father trained me how to take over a business. I worked with him every day. I took over the business.

4. What challenges did you face when building your business, and how did you overcome them? Did you come across any unique circumstances because of your race?

   I need a mentor, someone who can help marketing and give me a hand to build my strength up in that particular area by marketing, I mean I need someone to help me with buyers and a client base broader than my current African American urban faith-based customers. Marketing to help me obtain more corporate clients in need of pest control.

5. What types of support were most helpful to you when you were building your business? For example, did your local community play a role in shaping your business interests and development, or maybe it was a mentor? What or who was that one thing that made you believe, "Yes, I can do this!"

   My family and husband.

6. What do you think are the essential skills needed for African American entrepreneurs, to succeed in America? Also, what personal attitudes do you think are essential?

   Belief in oneself.

7. If you had the chance to start over again, would you do anything differently? More to the point, if you would, what's the reason?

   Get a proper education.

8. How would you characterize the state of African American entrepreneurship in the United States? For instance, is it in the early stages, is it growing, or is it mature? Do you think it is open to all or limited to certain individuals? Is it viable from anywhere in the country, or more favorable in certain states?

   The future for African American entrepreneurs is unknown.

9. Are you a member of any business organizations? Are these organizations unique to African Americans or open to all races? Did they contribute to your business success?

   Yes.

10. Do you think social networks and personal connections are important to business? Did you use networking when building your business, and are your social networks race-based?

    Yes.

11. If you could advise young African American entrepreneurs or other young people thinking about starting a business, what would be the most important thing, and why?

    Do not be afraid.

CHAPTER 4

Analysis of the Findings

Analysis is the critical starting point of strategic thinking.
—Kenichi Ohmae

The findings from the survey conducted by the authors provide a frame of reference on the mindset of African American entrepreneurs in America.

While the authors did not obtain responses from a broader demographic segment of African American entrepreneurs, the viewpoints shared by the entrepreneurs were highly insightful. The authors believe the findings are relevant to the academic and business communities as well as the general public. Government officials, international organizations, and think tanks can use some of the featured information to develop policies and programs.

Summary of Findings

In highlighting the findings, questions asked and common responses are highlighted. The authors then proceed to discuss the business implications using an assessment paragraph.

Listed below are our findings.

Question 1	Responses
Role of family in entrepreneurial decision	*Influenced by father, mother, siblings, grandparents, spouse and other relatives, and friends; a community/church leader; other entrepreneurs and role models; and a self-starter.*

Assessment of the Role of the Family in the Entrepreneurial Decision

The findings suggest that African American entrepreneurs tend to be influenced by those close to them such as family and friends. Community leaders and role models also yield some influence in the entrepreneurial decision. There are cases, however, where the African American entrepreneur had an innate passion for creating or building and decided to start an enterprise without any form of influence. Given that most of the respondents found family, friends, and community as an impetus for entrepreneurship suggest that those surrounding the African American entrepreneur can shape business decisions.

Question 2	Responses
Role of education in business success	*Education obtained included Associate degree, some college, Bachelor's degree, Master's degree, Law School, industry certification courses, and workshops; college drop-out; no formal education.*

Assessment of the Role of Education in Business Success

The findings from this research study suggest that African American entrepreneurs have a broad range of educational backgrounds ranging from little education to those with postgraduate degrees. It is evident that lack of formal education does not necessarily preclude one from entrepreneurial success. In further discussions with some of the respondents, a clear value was placed on education especially, formal, or informal education that can contribute to business knowledge and success. Some respondents cited the importance of taking part in academic and government-sponsored business development programs.

Question 3	Responses
What were the drivers and steps for the business start-up?	*Drivers included developmental programs (i.e., SBA workshops, business and programs, online classes, college); involvement in a family enterprise; career; mentor; family; networks; desire for independence; and incarceration.*

Assessment of the Drivers for Business Start-up

In the case of African American entrepreneurs, it appears that family, friends, and networks can stimulate entrepreneurial intent and the ultimate decision to start an enterprise. Similarly, experiential events such as education, training, and a career can lead to an entrepreneurial decision.

Self-motivation also stokes the entrepreneurial fire, especially in cases where the person seeks independence or financial betterment.

Question 4	Responses
Challenges faced when starting the business	*Challenges include: minority certification and qualification process; credit; access to capital and investors; marketing know-how; financial knowledge; business skills; lack of training and technology; access appropriate contacts; lack of mentors; networks outside minority community; finding key personnel (i.e., accountants, lawyers), regulatory changes; race; overcoming powerlessness; and criminal history.*

Assessment of Challenges Faced When Starting the Business

This research study found that African American entrepreneurs are confronted with numerous challenges when they start an enterprise. These challenges can be classified into six clusters: Knowledge (i.e., marketing and financial knowledge); Skills (i.e., specific training and technology), Capital (i.e., access to credit, capital and investors); Support (i.e., mentors and outside networks); Information (i.e., understanding certification process and knowing about regulatory changes); and Personal Barriers (racial and personal obstacles). Given the broad range of challenges, it is conceivable that even the most well-intentioned government or community support program could fail to discuss some areas needing help. In assisting the African American entrepreneur, the challenges need to be viewed holistically, and problems need to be discussed rather than merely in parts.

Question 5	Responses
Who provided support when building the business?	*When building the enterprise support were found from family members and friends; mentors; military experience; incarceration; past experiences; previous failures; Business Assistance Program; local and national organizations; unions and local trade organizations; academic supporters; acceptance by peers and competitors; franchisors; and capital access.*

Assessment on Support Providers When Building the Business

The findings suggest that African American entrepreneurs tend to benefit from multiple sources. Four support clusters are evident: (1) People (i.e., family, friends, mentors); (2) Experiences (i.e., military, incarceration, career, failures); (3) Community (i.e., local and national organizations, academe); and (4) Business (i.e., franchisor training, capital access). An African American entrepreneur who makes an effort to draw support from all of these four levels improves the chances of successfully building an enterprise.

Question 6	Responses
Essential skills and attitudes needed for business success in America	*Skills and attitudes essential for success include: independence; belief in oneself; communication; separating family and friends from business decisions; experience; financial management skills; human relations skills; enhancing employee talent and performance access to support; seeking and finding help; networking; acquiring information and knowledge; getting certified as a minority business; and understanding regulatory matters.*

Assessment of Essential Skills and Attitudes Needed for Success

The research findings suggest that in order for African American entrepreneurs to succeed in America, he or she needs to able to manage in three levels: Manage Oneself (i.e., independence, belief in oneself, valuable experiences, communicate effectively); Manage People (i.e., human relations, enhancing employee talent and performance); and Manage Environment (i.e., networking, finding help, acquiring information, and understanding regulatory matters). Acquiring and developing skills toward the understanding of these three levels can contribute to business success.

Question 7	Responses
Lessons learned, what would be done differently?	*The experiences include: obtaining education and training; learn through experience; take advice; enjoy life; leverage family and friends; find a mentor; do research and strategic planning; plan, share the business; know the laws and regulations; reinvest into the business.*

Assessment of the Main Business Lessons Learned

In analyzing the lessons African American entrepreneurs learned along the way, three tracks were evident: Developmental (relating to personal growth and development); Attitudinal (relating to attitudes and actions); and Strategic (relating to business activities to achieve a goal). Developmental lessons include obtaining education and training and learning through experience and advice. Attitudinal lessons include insights such as enjoying life and relationships with friends and family. Strategic lessons relate to the lessons learned in business that will shape future actions, for instance, plan, share the company, and know the rules and regulations among others. It is worth noting that lessons learned as well as the courses of action they decide to take can come in several forms.

Question 8	Responses
State of African American entrepreneurship in the United States	*Description on the state of African American entrepreneurship in the United States include: anchored on tradition; growing; alive and well; open to all; open to women minorities; favored with minority set-aside rulings; supported by federal, state, and local governments; opened up new opportunities, complicated; don't know; daunting challenges; lack market definition for minority markets; lack of support from minority groups; start-up difficult; federal, state, and local governments create road-blocks; lack capital access; many are small and have difficulty growing; entrepreneurs feel they are losing government support; and future is unknown.*

Assessment of the State of African American Entrepreneurship in the United States

The respondents' views on the state of African American entrepreneurship in the United States were mixed. Three types were observed—Optimist, Pragmatist, and Pessimist. The Optimist group felt the African American entrepreneurship is growing and has opened up doors to all, including women minorities. The Pragmatist group described the current situation flatly with comments such as many are small businesses and have difficulty growing and that the government at times creates roadblocks. The Pessimist group offered a negative view such as the loss of public support and uncertainty of the future. This finding suggests that the experiences, as well as the outlook of African American entrepreneurs in the United States, are diverse.

Question 9	Responses
Membership in business organizations and its role in success	*Out of 21 respondents, 16(76%) claimed that they were members of business organizations and found value in membership, 5(24%) did not see value in membership in the business organization and have opted not to be involved. Examples of the organizations they participated in include: education, civic, and professional groups; business assistance programs, networking organizations, mentoring organizations, guilds, fraternal organizations, alumni organizations, bar association, community organizations, Rotary club and civic groups, and golf and sports groups.*

Assessment of the Importance of Business Organizations

Findings suggest that African American entrepreneurs perceive the value of membership in business organizations in different ways. A vast majority find business organizations to be instrumental to their business success. This group has built business alliances and friendships in many forms of business, social, and civic organizations. The group that opted not to take part in business organizations chose to focus their social efforts on a close-knit network including friends, family, venture stakeholders, academia, and the community.

Question 10	Responses
Importance of social networks and networking for business success	*Out of 21 respondents, 11(52%) agreed that social networks contribute to business success, 6(29%) disagreed, and 4(19%) were unsure. Those that agreed cited the following reasons why they see value in networking: relevant to international business, critical to setting up contacts, opportunity to meet and learn, helps business, link to key players, and a fantastic way to find mentors. Those who disagreed indicated that the social aspect outweighs the business and can be distracting. Those who were unsure were ambivalent finding some social networking useful in some instances and useless in others.*

Assessment of the Importance of Social Networks

The findings suggest that African American entrepreneurs had different viewpoints on the value of social networks. A majority saw the value and found networks to be relevant to business success. Others believed that there are other more suitable methodologies one can pursue to grow an enterprise.

Question 11	Responses
Advice to young African American entrepreneurs and other entrepreneurs	*Advice to young African American entrepreneurs include: believe in yourself; follow your heart and passion; share; enjoy what you are doing; don't let failure define you; don't be afraid; follow your own path; stay in school; be educated; find a mentor stay involved; gather information yourself; ask questions and listen; know what you don't know; understand challenges you face; learn from others; attend free SBA workshops; seek help to solve problems; utilize tools available through business assistance programs, grants, laws, and regulations.*

Assessment of the Advice to Young African American Entrepreneurs

The advice the African American entrepreneurs offered to the younger generation were of three types: Attitudinal, Professional, and Practical. Attitudinal advice included comments such as believe in yourself and follow your heart and passion. Professional advice included statements such as stay in school, be educated, and find a mentor. Practical advice included insights such as use tools available through business assistance programs, grants, laws, and regulations. This advice was likely drawn from the entrepreneur considers firsthand experiences as essential to future business success.

The research findings point out to five important themes about African American entrepreneurship in America:

1. *High influence of friends and family*—The results of the investigation suggest that friends and relatives played a significant role in the entrepreneurial decision. Among the drivers for business start-ups, friends, and family were also cited as an influencer. When discussing support systems and individuals when building their business, again several respondents cited the importance of family, extended family, and friends. This study confirms that friends and family factors into the African American enterprise.
2. *Education is important and should be aligned with needs*—Education was cited as important by several respondents, particularly since drivers for start-up and support for building the business. However, when queried on the challenges faced when starting the

business education-related knowledge were cited as necessary (i.e., marketing, financial, business skills). There appears to be some gap in the education some of the entrepreneurs acquired as compared to the knowledge needed to manage and business assistance programs, workshops, and formal entrepreneurial educational opportunties, and provider focusing on concerns unique and business development needs of African American entrepreneurs. It is noteworthy that as advice to young entrepreneurs, some respondents suggested staying in school and getting educated.

3. *A multitude of challenges*—The research study found multiple difficulties confronting African American entrepreneurs. The challenges faced when starting a business including Knowledge, Skills, Capital, Support, Information, and Personal Barriers. Given that the African American community is a key contributor to the U.S. economy, government institutions need to understand and address these challenges in a holistic manner rather than on a piecemeal basis. A comprehensive plan of action needed.

4. *Management ability is essential across several levels*—When queried on the core competencies required for success, management across three tiers was noted—Management of Self, Management of People, and Management of Environment. Given the high impact management ability has on the future success of the African American entrepreneur, developmental initiatives in these areas are worthwhile investments. African entrepreneurs would be served well by planning their personal and professional growth and development along the lines of these management levels.

5. *Engagement and relevance to the community*—The African American community deeply woven into the economic fabric of the United States. The success of African American entrepreneurs benefits not only the African Americans but the entire country. African American entrepreneurs and the U.S. economy have a symbiotic relationship. When both parties are actively engaged, a win–win scenario emerges. The research findings suggest that majority of African American entrepreneurs are actively involved in business organizations and social networks, including community programs. The entrepreneurs receive help from it, and so do the community and

the U.S. economy. Strengthening this synergistic relationship would stimulate economic growth in locations throughout the United States.

These findings point out to the active engagement of African American entrepreneurs in contemporary America. Despite obstacles, they have taken on an active entrepreneurial agenda throughout the country. They made a valiant effort to pursue the American dream and contribute to the prosperity and success of the nation.

CHAPTER 5

Conclusion and Discussion

In literature and life, we ultimately pursue, not conclusions, but beginnings.

—Sam Tanenhaus

This book brings into focus the entrepreneurial thinking of the African American entrepreneur and their understanding of their uneasy interactions with mainstream America, their daily activities as a business owner, and the road they travel between home and work, the community and jobs, and church on Sunday.

In this book, entrepreneurship defined as a person engaged gathering resources to create and build a business enterprise by using creativity, risk, and innovation (Harwood 1982). Limited are the studies on African American entrepreneurship. There is a need for a deeper exploration into the mindset and motivation of this subsector (Reddit.com 2017). Inclusion is an important angle. In the words of Verna Myers (2017): "Diversity is being invited to the party, inclusion is being asked to dance."

Past studies and research on African American entrepreneurship point out to an ethnic group facing certain limitations.

African American entrepreneurs pursue just-in-time strategies, and are calculated risk-takers with creative and innovative flair. They are working long hours following their American dream. When African Americans start a new business, or pursue the ownership of an existing company, they begin a journey on a road filled with curves designed to challenge all entrepreneurs regardless of race. They interact daily, gathering resources they need as an entrepreneur. They explore in new opportunities. They establish business relationships inside and outside of their community, targeting, connecting, and interacting with mainstream America and African American entrepreneurs. The negotiate two separate and distinct business environments. They also insulate their entrepreneurial journey with African American traditions.

It is indisputable that African American entrepreneurs pursuing the American dream will invariably encounter obstacles as they gather the resources necessary to own and operate a sustainable business. They are at risk based on assumptions and stereotypes and the disregard for African Americans, the unintended migrant.

The African Americans interviewed in this research are rooted in traditions passed down from generation to generation by their ancestors. Social and cultural history taught them to systematically reflect survival without on the resources they do not and cannot access or control. The understand making a way out of no way is the only way to survive the entrepreneurial journey.

Insights on Entrepreneurial History

One set of questions in the entrepreneurial interview pertained to entrepreneurial history. Respondents were asked: "Kindly provide an overview of the family history. For example, was there an entrepreneur in the household? Did the family history influence the decision to start a business?"

These questions intended to establish the relevance of social history (Captains log 2017). According to Juliet E. K. Walker (1999), during slavery, African American males operated as entrepreneurs in the construction industry, often as slave managers supervising other slaves. Some even had the authority to negotiate contracts. Women slaves worked through the night, sewing, washing, and ironing clothes. They paid a portion of their salary to their mistress.

African Americans historically proved their ability survive and provide economic sustainability through entrepreneurship. When they arrived in America, they found themselves propelled into self-employment during slavery. They did not pursue the American dream; they focused on survival and economic sustainability. They supported their family and community. They gathered and distributed resources for their basic needs, food, and shelter. Through self-employment, they quickly learned they had an opportunity to interconnect the channels for their survival through faith, family, community, and economic stability. As descendants of former slaves, like many others throughout history, they learned how to survive in a hostile environment. They quickly became tradesmen, primary service providers to former slave owners, and migrating north with specific skills in carpentry, housework, cooking, farming, construction, and artist and entertainers. They learned how to barter, exchange services, take a calculated risk, and survive.

The family social history and deeply rooted desire to survive exerts a powerful influence on African American entrepreneurs, and are the primary source they draw the strength from to take a calculated risk and travel the winding road of uncertainty. With entrepreneurship come many frustrations as one attempts to transform entrepreneurial dreams into successful enterprises.

Insights on Business Assistance

Another group of questions explored the importance of seeking professional help. Questions asked included: Are African American entrepreneurs members of professional business organizations? Are these groups unique to African Americans or open to all races? Did they contribute to the success?

One of the interviewees offered interesting insights. As an African American, female, New York City artist, she is accomplished in her field and has assimilated well into her profession and community. She shares how difficult it is to rationalize the critics reviewing her work and their seeming need to describe her as "the African American artist" not simply "the artist." She goes on to say, "it seems obvious, my identification and qualifications as an artist, purposes and success are not based solely on my talent alone, my race is also a factor." In her late seventies, the feedback is a current reality. The artist skillfully intertwined her race with her art. Sadly, the consequences of mainstream American's assumptions concerning the strengths and weakness of an artist based on her race impacts her morale, psyche, and consequently her art. She expressed her concern that mainstream America's intertwining the descendants of slaves with professional deficiencies are damaging. The assumption would have a profound impact on whether she achieves anything as an artist. She was not in denial about race issues. She merely wanted to succeed as an artist regardless of her race.

In this interview, the interviewee stressed the importance of support. In her view, African American artists who had positive experiences early in their community seemingly learn to use race as an adjustment in their lifestyle and understanding of mainstream America. They are more flexible and are prepared to make adaptations more readily than artists who not share similar experiences. The profile for this artist certainly stresses the need for feedback and support focused on art and not race. Artist-entrepreneurs require honest and constructive feedback during their development phase and the launching of their ventures. They need approval for their artistry, not their race.

One interviewee operated funeral homes. The owner linked success to the family's ability to develop trust with their clients and establish a good reputation throughout the community. During the interview, the owner shared how trust is the first set of norms in their value system and the resulting healthy personal relationships with individuals and families in the community.

A couple whom the authors interviewed further highlighted the relevance of building business credibility among professional groups and in the community. The couple owned a small chain of fast food carry-out restaurants located in an African American neighborhood, as well as predominately white shopping plaza in a small city in Midwest. Despite having different customer bases, the community credibility, professionalism, and personalized relationships led to their business success.

While researching, the authors came across the story of an admirable African American entrepreneur. While the authors were not able to interview him, his story is worthwhile sharing. His name is Dr. William Pickard, and he was the founder, chairperson, and chief executive officer (CEO) of Global Automotive Alliance, one of the country's leading minority-owned businesses. Under his leadership, the company became the first minority-owned group of plastic-parts to service the top three U.S. automakers (Reference for Business, 2017). On several occasions, the company was on *Black Enterprise's* list of the top 100 industrial/service companies (Referenceforbusiness.com 2017). Pickard was honored numerous times for his business acumen, actions to assist African Americans and other minorities in the business world, and commitment to teaching and mentoring others. He has a history of cooperation with mainstream America. From Pickard's story, it is noteworthy that William Pickard strategized and conducted business across all racial lines. He attracted, selected, and maintained relationships with mainstream American business and successfully made them allies and partners.

Insights on Social Networks

The third set of questions sought to explore the importance of networks in African American businesses. Questions asked included: Do you think social networks and personal connections are important to business? Did you use networking when building your business, and are your social networks race-based?

All respondents recognized the elements of support from the African American community in their business ventures. All respondents also referenced the importance of friendship not only in the African American community but also the nonminority business owners, professionals.

In the African American community, networks of immediate and extended families, social circles, professional organizations, religious and political groups interact forming agents of support that are both visible and invisible. They serve as the collective social capital. These cumulative support bases in the community are avenues for networking and social learning.

Some of the groups are more stable with built-in reinforcements that mold them. The community networks are understood as a necessity for positive reinforcement. The entrepreneurs interviewed in this book confirmed the importance of the community groups and how they interconnect as a support network for trust, reciprocity, and emotional intelligence. Academic literature reinforces the need for networks, social capital, and emotional intelligence. After slavery, according to E. K. Walker (1999), they filled a void in the South left behind by the white men migrating north, pursuing opportunities in factories in the industrial North.

The factors shaping African American entrepreneurship are extensive, varied, and often ignored. The viewpoints of African American entrepreneurs interviewed in this book linked a range of factors to their success or failure. From the interviews, it has been clear that while entrepreneurial drive offers a framework for success, social, economic, political, and geographic circumstances, social learning histories and race-based assumptions are important intervening factors. The consequences of these intervening and often interrelated factors can lead to what was described earlier as the boomerang effect. These external factors reach into past American values and America's future. Through the questions and interviews, the authors recognized the centrality of the entrepreneurs' social learning history while underscoring the channels that connect the business owner's race and business opportunities to continuous boomerang effects.

The African American entrepreneurs' ability to succeed is impacted by their race, social learning history, and the state, local, and federal executive orders, laws, regulations, and public policies mandating race-based inclusion and participation among others. Understanding these issues and taking proactive measures will result in America's overcoming racial disparities in countless small businesses across the country.

Finally, race-based assumptions, stereotypes, oral history, storytelling, and social history shapes the willingness and strength of the African American entrepreneur to take a calculated risk when doing business on the playing field set-aside for minorities. In America, history alongside intervening factors propels a socio-economic and business boomerang that affects the African American entrepreneurial dream. Managing the velocity, the distance, and the power of this boomerang on their enterprise is a daily struggle confronting African Americans in America.

Insights on Community Engagement

One set of questions considered the extent of community participation, which leads to questions such as: "How engaged are you in the community? Do you think social networks and personal connections are important to business? Did you use networking when building your business? Are your social networks race-based?"

A few entrepreneurs interviewed begun to use golf as a tool for networking with bankers, lawyers, accountants, and mainstream American business owners. Some entrepreneurs indicated that they used the golf course as a networking venue to conduct business and develop partnerships with mainstream business owners and to mentor young African

Americans. The entrepreneurs took part in various programs that teach golf, offer college scholarships and networks participants with universities and colleges that offer golf scholarships to African American youth. They use the game as a business networking tool and youth development opportunity and duality on their terms.

Membership in private golf clubs is by invitation only. As a result, the race and gender of the African American entrepreneur become the ethos for access to networking opportunities with mainstream America. While the number of African American members in private country clubs has grown, the numbers do not reflect the numbers of African American golfers proportionately. The founders of NNGA filled the void by launching a national chain golf club open to all ages. They also became major donors to young African Americans attending college. They maintained direct involvement in the community. There has been active participation in diverse community activities and events, indicating an active inclusion in mainstream American social life and events for a select few. A considerable number of entrepreneurs interviewed networked socially and professionally as members of African American sororities, fraternities, the Masonic Masons, Eastern Stars, National Association of Black Engineers, National Black MBA Association, United Construction Workers Association, and churches other private membership organizations as the primary source for networking and support.

The owners expressed the importance of community engagement and memberships in business organizations. The owners view memberships as a networking tool and contributors to the growth and development of their businesses.

Participation in religious activities appears to be the norm. 97 percent of the respondents were members of faith-based organizations. Approximately 73 percent stated that they attend church on a regular basis.

Community engagement and networking do not come easy for some African American entrepreneurs because of the social stratification and geographic boundaries supporting African Americans. For some, the inability to develop mainstream American social networks, receive information about opportunities promptly, and identify qualified independent resources, lead to a competitive disadvantage.

Insights on African American Women Entrepreneurs

Duality in lifestyle and business is a contemporary reality. For example, African American women entrepreneurs are expected to assimilate into the "mainstream American woman's" perspective of gender while maintaining their "roots" in the African American culture. Often, the scenario results in two separate and distinct business zones for these women: race and gender.

African American women entrepreneurs need to conduct business in many cases to survive and provide for their families. A myriad of factors influences their ability to conduct business. These factors include: (a) their ability to self-regulate and understand the duality of the zones given the social and economic situational cues imposed by the external business and personal environment at every intersection of their entrepreneurial activities from the kitchen table to the office; (b) the timing of external resource availability; (c) the cultural contexts for women entrepreneurs; and (d) the necessity and importance of African American women in the African American community.

These factors show that African American female entrepreneurs are outsiders seeking to get into the business and social worlds of white men, women and African American men. These African American women are still outsiders during their encounters because race and gender invalidate options. Their personal business and personal lens are clouded, and in some cases undermined by duality. As African American women in An America, they could not: (a) control the external environmental gender-based stereotypes framework; (b) understand the illusions based on the assumptions about African American women; or (c) trust in mainstream American women based on their shared views about gender. African American women entrepreneurs are expected to engage in two designated business zones' the interviews with African American female entrepreneurs, it was clear that responses to each question were different. Each entrepreneur processed questions differently. The responses were linked to the type of business owned. They articulated thoughts in a distinctive manner. Answers came from various directions and emerged in diverse paths because they were driven by different social histories, age, education, gender, and business industry, and access to information. Each entrepreneur has her own story. Insights on resource availability and constraint; business revenue and succeed; Black American entrepreneurs need adequate education, work experience, and training, and capital access (Bates 1996).

Countless African American business owners are trying to live their entrepreneurial dream. However, they encounter inequities in areas such as access to capital, union apprenticeship training programs, mentors linked directly to their social status, race, ethnicity, religion, and business industry. The inequities are frequently driven by stereotypes and assumptions, require the African American to "live the dream" of becoming an entrepreneur in a designated enterprise zone filled with inequities. The designated enterprise zone frequently dims the meaning of entrepreneurship and economic sustainability. The African American entrepreneur has situational cues and situational awareness are continuously linked to the consequence of the inequities and unrealistic perceptions and assumptions. One entrepreneur interviewed succinctly captured in words the pursuit of his elusive dream, "going from one generation to the next generation, passing the baton, understanding how business changes, while trying to grow the business, you miss a lot because of access to resource difficulties."

Insights on Business Adaptation and Transformation

African American entrepreneurs are expected to adapt, reinvent, and transform their businesses into successful ventures. An interviewed male African American entrepreneur, who was a role model for success in his community for a decade, expresses his experience with duality in his life and business. During the interview, he reflected on the countless changes that took place in the minority business settings over the years and the response by mainstream America. He emphasized the fact that it is important to stay abreast of changes that are taking place in the local and national settings. He keeps track of politically driven transformations, challenges, regulations, and race-based stereotypes that daily impact his ability to access business opportunities and to succeed in his chosen profession. Business adaptations need to take place promptly. The interviewed entrepreneur demonstrated his ability to respond to the transformations quickly. He emphasized the need for reflective and adaptive skills. He understood the importance of interacting and communicating with mainstream American trade union representatives and many companies' business. That included employee policy to reduce and correct the distortions linked to inequities. In his business, he developed a framework for the just-in-time (JIT) knowledge and strategies in response to situational cues he acquired from his environment. He noted the relevance of prompt information gathering to prepare for and make sound decisions based on the accurate assessment of the business situation. Business is a constant quest for best performance. He mentioned the use of temporary assimilation as an entrepreneur in the designated enterprise zone to be able to succeed in his enterprise and "live the dream." As learned from this case, African American entrepreneurs need to know the business environment well, and plan the need to be flexible and nimble to navigate challenges and grasp opportunities quickly (Referenceforbusiness.com 2017).

The interviewed entrepreneur understood the environmental inequities and the need to work with situational cues necessary for the adaptation and assimilation of the business. Other entrepreneurs interviewed had different life experiences, but displayed similar capacity for business transformation through situational cues and awareness.

Several entrepreneurs interviewed actively engaged in changing their business practices. They were not passive entrepreneurs. They constantly seek current information that can potentially transform their businesses. They interacted actively with mainstream America. They adapted, assimilated, and transformed and converted their operations of activities. They felt compelled to try to understand, accommodate, and adapt their strategies constantly to deal with never-ending changes in government regulations and race-based stereotypes. They follow their innate survival instincts.

Insights on Growing the Enterprise

A business enterprise goes through various stages of development. Each stage brings about a distinct set of challenges and opportunities.

While there are similar enterprise experiences among mainstream entrepreneurs and African American entrepreneurs, the social history along with external influencing factors such as access to capital, location, and business development support often leads the African American entrepreneur into a different path. For instance, during the start-up phases, limited awareness of their ability binds African American entrepreneurs to succeed in the majority controlled small business environment. As they progress as a business entrepreneur, they reflect and rely on the JIT knowledge and strategies generated through their situational awareness during the growth stage of their business.

Brief descriptions of the African American entrepreneurs interviewed by the authors include the following:

Food Manufacturer

This business succeeds because of the United States Department of Defense minority requirements, mandating inclusion minority vendors. There was capital access for minority-owned enterprises. He operated the business around the world and networked with his peers as a member of a national African American sorority. The company also owns a female-owned minority subsidiary.

Entertainment Center Operator

The owner became one of the original African American owners of entertainment venues in an urban community. This couple owned a bowling alley and a club in the early 1960s. The club hosted African American entertainers. While not mentioned in historical documentaries, they are recognized as an unsung hero. He attended a historically black university, joined the military, and started working for the small business as a teenager. Bowling became a part of his lifestyle and a business networking platform. He became the first African American in 1964 to appear on the "Championship Bowling" TV show. After marriage, he and his wife became an entrepreneurial team. Their entertainment venues were fundraisers, dancing, and food. In later years, they started an urban garden, giving the food to local community residents. They also started a program to teach the youth of the community how to become entrepreneurs. This couple methodically explored strategies that would enhance and stabilize the African American community; they developed a venue that served as a networking location for leaders in the African American community. The success was rooted in their ability to make something out of nothing.

Construction Manager/Contractor

This entrepreneur is a male and was born in Cleveland, Ohio. He graduated magna cum laude from undergraduate school and immediately attended law school. He is currently President and CEO of a major construction company. He is a third-generation entrepreneur operating the business in multiple states. The company began in the early 1950s. The success of this business is not based on race and mandates for inclusion and access to set-aside opportunities. The success is based on standards of excellence starting in the office and continuing construction site and union construction workforce. The owner is a strong contemporary leader, advocating inclusion and diversity and collaboration.

The demands of the changing business phases force the African American entrepreneur to take on a new awareness and action agenda. During the business start-up phase, African American entrepreneurs do not view the designated business playing fields as difficult. They see the field as an opportunity to pursue the "dream." During the growth stage, they begin to learn through situational cues and situational awareness, the control of compulsive acts of survival and calculated risk-taking. They learned how to respond to the boomerang effect of inequities assimilation. They start to understand the importance of race and ethnicity situational cues. They realize that business is not aligned with expectations because of the harness controlling the African American entrepreneur. They make the adjustments required to throttle their competencies and capabilities, as they engage and pursue business opportunities on their designated business enterprise zone. They learn that if they are going "live the dream," they must draw on their social learning history, emotional intelligence, and social capital, and the power of the heritage and social history as self-employed.

Accurate situational assessment along with active network support can support the business as they move to the next level. Many entrepreneurs draw upon religion to help overcome stumbling blocks and overcome difficult challenges. They understand the importance of drawing logical conclusions and strategic planning. They see the need to collaborate with the bankers, mentors, advocates, and business allies among mainstream American entrepreneurs. They value the importance of information access and know its critical link to success. They face operational limitations and external challenges and work through the issues. They learn to translate situational cues associated with mainstream American race-based events and experiences and take the necessary steps toward adaptation, transformation, integrating storytelling and real-world experiences. They learn to navigate the illusions of small business ownership and success into the realities associated with the world of the African American in America. The process and stages for any entrepreneur's development is a part of the growth process and is closely linked to the evolving business environment.

Insights on the Development of African American Entrepreneur

The authors sought to examine workable approaches in developing the African American entrepreneur.

In one case, an African American mayor of a major city took an interest in helping an African American entrepreneur, who was an ex-offender, successfully transition back into the community. The mayor hosted weekly open walk-in meetings with his constituency on a first-come basis. The entrepreneur stood in line for a month to see the mayor and make a request for assistance. He asked the Mayor to negotiate with the trade unions, and help him enroll in an apprenticeship program. The mayor arranged this opportunity for him. After completing the apprentice program, he was hired by minority construction company. While incarcerated in a maximum security prison along with with his family upbringing taught him to remain focused, work hard, never return to prison and eventually open his businesses. Today, he is a master plumber and the owner of a successful HVAC company.

There are several effective development programs available for African American entrepreneurs. In the case of the ex-offender interested in starting a business, the Commission on African America Males programs ex-offenders the focused re-entry, business development training and education. Accordingly, they stressed the importance of an effective plan of activities and milestones generated to support accountability as citizens in the community and self-directed development of small businesses.

The programs also focused on social learning, and empowerment through entrepreneurship.

The framework for minority business development programs is designed to engage the owner in an active learning process. The materials provide organized information customized for African American entrepreneurs. The information is not dependent on perceptual arrays of race-based assumptions concerning the capability of minority business owners to succeed. The programs provide options based on the entrepreneurs need to know,and varying levels of generality and abstractions. They vary from simple to complex strategies for successful business development in the designated race and gender zone and mainstream America. The framework for minority small business development programs takes different forms including scripts linked to race and gender; categories and doing business in America designed to generate lifelong entrepreneurs and learners from the golf course to their business. They are not traditional small business development workshops.

In 2017 there are countless business developmental and entrepreneurial training programs offered by the government, the Small Business Association, and local community colleges and universities. Through the web, training videos and even free online courses in entrepreneurship and various business topics are available.

The successful development of an African American entrepreneur must go beyond the mere use of training programs. It should be focused on areas for critical development. Developmental needs would also vary from one entrepreneur and another. For instance, in the case of the ex-offender, aside from business and social-psychological development, introduction to economic development connections upon his arrival in the disadvantaged urban community proved to be helpful. The needed training and recognition of his potential as a contributor, not a distracter, to the community, resulted in a collaboration between the providers of service, who were concerned about his "thinking" and ability to view his options through a personal lens and negotiate the path ahead.

A multifaceted support system would be necessary. The development of African American entrepreneurs also needs to put in context intervening factors such as social class, race, ethnicity, and religion. These factors have frequently been defined with inequities. Examining key theoretical approaches enables an understanding of entrepreneurial development from a broad perspective. It sets the stage for the identification of inequities (e.g., social class, race, ethnicity, religion, education skills training, and status in the community), solving problems, and setting up a pathway for the development of the entrepreneur. The entrepreneurs interviewed aimed to become or to still be influential members of the community. They understood the value of growth and development and the key role it plays in entrepreneurial survival in America.

Insights on Coping with Change

In all businesses, change is a given. African American entrepreneurs need to deal with shifts the organizations, competitors, markets, customers, and communities continue to evolve.

During one interview, an African American entrepreneur recounted how federal legislation generated situational cues that automatically labeled his business opportunities with massive amounts of regulations. He was unprepared for the changes. He was also taken aback by reactions from mainstream America that supported the changes. He vowed to be carefully attuned to political and market changes from thereon. As a result, his business is one of the most successful, not only in his home state but also in other countries.

An area where many African American entrepreneurs stay unprepared and confused is the duality of their business. The entrepreneurs are sometimes baffled on why policies are not applicable to all and are not applied consistently.

Changes have taken many forms. As their enterprises developed, the business and the entrepreneur changed. These changes occurred in both their social and business environments. The entrepreneurs are shored up by their social learning history mindset to operate a business in two separate and distinct worlds. They cited duality as a major factor in their success or failure. Many entrepreneurs, however, were unclear about the reasons and operational framework surrounding this duality. Some did not see the linkage between social history and their cultural values. Others inadvertently developed mistaken conclusions on the reasons behind inequities in their social status, race, and ethnicity.

African American entrepreneurs need to be able to deal with personal, organizational, and external changes that are taking place. They need to be able to dig deep, understand their strengths and competencies well, and draw upon relevant cultural contexts to manage change well.

Insights in Entrepreneurial Theories

The theories of entrepreneurship are static or dynamic. They are based on current and historical events that are linked to the mainstream An America's view of entrepreneurship. As a result, theories are interconnected to race, and ethnicity based on stereotypes and assumptions about the African American entrepreneur. The entrepreneurial theories are often statements, explaining the relationship between one or more occurrences.

During the research, the authors did not feel prepared to advance specific theories on African American entrepreneurship. The data gathered is inadequate in forming over-generalizations or generalizations about African American entrepreneurship. The value and essence of this research endeavor lie in bringing forth the voices and insights of real-life African American entrepreneurs. The authors hope that these insights reinforce some of the theories that are being developed on the subject. It is hoped that this effort inspires others to explore the subject deeply.

More importantly, the authors hope that the insights offered inspiration to African American and other minority entrepreneurs to follow their entrepreneurial dreams and not become the victims of the winding road to success.

There were some lessons that stood out during the research. The authors understood the impact of discrimination, mandated inclusion, and the designated business playing field. They also recognized the importance of access to resources for the success of African American ventures. The viewpoints and profiles generated a lens into entrepreneurs regardless of race, ethnicity, or gender, share the same motivation and desire to achieve the American dream as entrepreneurs and economic sustainability. The authors explored the interconnection between the elements and parts of the laws, regulations, and legislation that appear to harness the African American entrepreneurs. The harness pushes the business and entrepreneur forward and pulls them backward. The entrepreneurs understood America's history and the history of their ancestors, the unwilling immigrants. The challenges force changes that are often linked to a transformation pathway of diversity and inclusion mandated by laws, regulations, and legislation, not acceptance of difference by mainstream America as an unpleasant fact. As African American entrepreneurs, they developed an understanding of the linkages between the chain of events linked to the inequities related to their social status, race, ethnicity, and regulations. The ability to process this understanding, while managing change and embracing transformations holds the key to entrepreneurial success.

Insights on the African American Entrepreneurial Playing Field

Interviews with many African American entrepreneurs gave snapshots of the African American entrepreneurial landscape. To supplement the interviews, the authors researched other angles that could shed light on the entrepreneurs' operational terrain.

The research conducted has confirmed the struggles faced by the African American entrepreneurs. It also showed that many have overcome these struggles and have become significant contributors to the American economy. As of 2012, receipts generated by black-owned businesses were at $150.2 billion (Blackdemographics.com 2017).

There exists an opportunity to increase the participation of African Americans in business in the United States. While African Americans constitute about 12.8 percent of the United States population, only about 5 percent of United States firms are owned by African Americans (United States Census Bureau 2007). In 2012, there were 2.6 million black-owned firms. The annual revenues of black-owned businesses at $187.6 billion stays insignificant compared to white-owned businesses ($12.9 trillion), Asian-owned businesses ($793.5 billion), and Hispanic-owned businesses ($473.6 billion) (Blackdemographics.com 2017).

The overall importance of minority business in America is growing. A study by Lowery (2004) showed that the share of minority-owned businesses increased from 21 percent in 1982 to 32 percent in 2002. The average receipts of minority-owned firms are $196,000 (US

Department of Commerce 2015). Black-owned businesses increased by 34.5 percent between 2007 and 2012 and number about 2.6 million (Blackdemographics.com 2017).

It is important to note that while minority firms are about 12 percent of U.S. businesses, their characteristics cannot be classified as one homogenous sector (SBA 2005; Cardon et al. 2008). For instance, Scott (1993) observed that minority firms performed similarly to nonminority companies about profitability, indebtedness, and liquidity. In the United States, there are about eight million minority-owned businesses, and their growth has been faster than nonminority-owned firms (US Department of Commerce 2015).

Despite operational challenges arising from their background and environmental problems, many enterprises have been created by African American and black entrepreneurs. A study on African American companies conducted by Sonfield (1986) noted that African American operations tend to be neither national nor regional, tend to work in one location catering to a market with a niche product or service, and tend not to be multiproduct. In the United States, the states that had the most black-owned businesses were District of Columbia (34.8 percent), Mississippi (27.7 percent), and Georgia (27.6 percent) (Black demongraphics.com 2017).

Information gathered from the entrepreneur interviews show that African American enterprises are typically in sectors such as construction/contracting, and distributors, media, cosmetics, entertainment, computer service/retailing, food/beverage wholesale and retail, miscellaneous manufacturing, and diverse services. Research showed that in 2012, 4 in 10 black-owned businesses or 1.1 million were in health care, social assistance, and other services such as repair, maintenance, personal, and laundry services (Blackdemographics.com 2017).

Across the United States, there are 2.58 million black-owned businesses, which generate $150 billion in annual revenue and employ 3.56 million people. Entrepreneurship not only helps business owners and their employees gain income, but it also has broader impacts. As inequality widens in the United States, entrepreneurship provides a pathway to building critical assets to bridge the economic divide (Knight 2017). Especially for African Americans, whose wealth was concentrated in housing and consequently lost much of their wealth in the wake of the Great Recession, business ownership is a way to rebuild wealth. The effects of entrepreneurship ripple through the community, helping to create jobs, spur innovation, and generate community wealth.

A recent report by the Association for Enterprise Opportunity (AEO), The Tapestry of Black Business Ownership in America: Untapped Opportunities for Success (Aeoworks 2017) shows that black business owners tend to be wealthier than their peers who are not business owners. The median net worth of black business owners is 12 times higher than that of nonbusiness owners, even factoring for those who began with more wealth.

In recent years, the sectors engaged by African American and black entrepreneurs have evolved. In a 30-year analysis conducted by Sonfield (2007) into the performance of the top 100 black enterprises, it was noted that sales volume had increased dramatically from $684 million in 1974 to over $19 billion in 2004. In this study, the following changes were observed in the number of enterprises engaged business sectors: Auto dealership (24 to 41), Food/Beverage Wholesale/Retail (19 to 11), Miscellaneous Manufacturing (12 to 11), Construction/Contracting (18 to 2), Media (7 to 6), Miscellaneous Services/Distribution (12 to 17), Energy (3 to 1), Health care and Cosmetics (2 to 0), Entertainment (3 to 0), Technology (0 to 11).

There are commonalities among minority enterprises. For instance, due to a variety of factors, many minority entrepreneurs are disadvantaged (De Freitas 1991). Many minority entrepreneurs are driven to start their businesses because of need (Bates 1997). Minority-owned businesses tend to be rooted in labor-intensive industries, and positioned in low-growth sectors (Robb 2002). Growth, however, in minority-owned firms have been significant. In the period 2007–2012, minority business enterprises grew by 39 percent from 5.8 million to 8 million (US Department of Commerce 2015).

The African American entrepreneurs interviewed experience tensions in finding work and family balance. The participants in the survey showed that the nuclear and extended family unit is of primary importance in the choices they make in the business and life. In fact, many reflective interviews reported that they lived in multigenerational and extended family households with members of the household being employed by the entrepreneur and the status of the business contributes to the economic sustainability of the family unit. The interview findings were consistent with research on minority entrepreneurship, which showed that the family unit is valued and is of primary importance in life (Lynch and Hanson 2004) and that many minority groups tend to have multigenerational and extended family households (Kamo 2000).

Insights into 2017 Challenges

In the surveys and the interviews, the entrepreneurs reflected on the constraints they experienced such as lack of access to management support and technology. From conversations, it was noted that most of the young African American college-educated management majors are not interested in working for African American business entities if the owner did not have a degree or have an extensive business history. Also considered in their employment decision are business growth opportunities beyond designated or segregated business zones. Many young African Americans are discouraged with the lack of access to capital and banking relationships in African American firms. Black American business is often constrained by lack of capital and weak banking relationships, which leads to business failures (Bates 1996). However, despite these obstacles, black-owned businesses employed 975,052 people with a payroll of about $27.7 billion (Blackdemographics.com 2017).

Minority entrepreneurs may experience high stress in their business endeavors. Minority entrepreneurs tend to spend considerable time in their activities and have higher workload compared to traditional entrepreneurs (Harris et al. 1999).

Much of African American youths have experienced challenges early in life and this sometimes leads to future constraints. For instance, dropout of black youth is at a rate that is twice that of the white (U.S. Census Bureau 2004). Black young people are less prone to be acquainted with small business owners as compared to white youth (Walstad and Kourilsky 1998). There are also added limitations about parental role models and education. Many blacks do not have a parent who is engaged in business (Hout and Rosen 2000). Studies have shown that only about 23 percent

percent of black entrepreneurs have a college degree compared to 30 percent in white businessmen (Fairlie 2004).

Many African American enterprises work in segregated markets, and these poses added challenges. Challenges associated with reliance on segregated markets include market size limitations, poorer consumers, high insurance, the risk of theft, and lack of access to credit and capital (Tabb 1970). African American entrepreneurs who rely on segregated markets are likely to fail (Brimmer and Terrell 1971).

Finding suitable role models and mentors in their social network may be scarce. Socioeconomic conditions in black communities can serve as a deterrent to finding inspiring entrepreneurial models (Rhodes and Butler 2004).

Lack of resources in business organizations and relevant institutions may limit their ability to network and grow their business. Poorer and less developed institutional frameworks among black communities restrict the success of business organizations (Rhodes and Butler 2004).

These combined set of challenges may have impeded the ability of African American entrepreneurs to succeed. The enterprises tend to have a higher likelihood of closing as compared to white businesses (Robb 2002). The rate of long-term success of African Americans and minority groups tend to be lower than whites (Hocker 2005). Lowrey (2004) observed that minority-owned businesses tend to have lower survival rates than nonminority businesses. The owned enterprises trailed white-owned businesses in the areas of sales, profits, and employee number (Fairlie and Robb 2007).

Many of the entrepreneurs interviewed voiced several of these challenges. It is remarkable that many have opted to deal with these difficulties head-on and turn them into opportunities to succeed.

Insights on Minority Business Opportunities

During the interviews, the authors were impressed with the African American entrepreneurs' innate ability to manage difficulties and create new opportunities for success. They fail, get up, dust themselves, put a plan together, and go for it. They are expert opportunity finders and creators. They are natural risk takers and survivors.

While there are countless business challenges that constrain African American entrepreneurs, some exciting opportunities exist. In the years 2007–2012, black-owned businesses increased by 34.5 percent (Black-demographics.com 2017).

The African American youth hold much promise. Black youth tend to be more interested in entrepreneurship as compared to the white youth (Wilson et al. 2004).

There is a strong predisposition toward entrepreneurship. Black men are one-third more likely to be self-employed as compared to white men (Fairlie 1999). African Americans are more apt to attempt to start a business than other ethnic groups (Kollinger and Minniti 2006).

The pursuit of financial betterment is high on the African American agenda. In the list of goals and motivational factors driving African Americans' financial goals were ranked 7th (Lee et al. 1996). The interviews and research show that African Americans look after each other. Black entrepreneurs tend to employ African Americans and other minority groups compared to white businessmen (Bates 1994). Black-owned businesses create about one million jobs, which can employ 4 percent of the working-age black population and provide a check for $7,000 every year for every working-age black American (Blackdemographics.com 2017).

African American entrepreneurs are ready, willing, and able to leverage what they should to succeed. Lee et al. (1996) noted that African Americans tend to be motivated by using skills, venture creation, control over life, and achievement of the desired lifestyle. The drive for finding value and converting them into workable business opportunities have been observed in several entrepreneurs interviewed.

There is a powerful sense of community. Racial enclaves offer solidarity and enhance business development (Cummings 1980). In Black communities, religious groups offered anchors for business development and training (Fratoe 1986). With enhanced social networking and solidarity, ethnic groups gain abilities to better process information, expand financial capacity, strengthen market power, built trust, and build customer relationships (Light and Rosenstein 1995). The interviews showed that the interviewed entrepreneurs were active in their communities and were ready to help and mentor others.

Many successful African American entrepreneurs worked with all types of businesses regardless of the competitive race to grow their enterprises. The interviews underscored the importance of networking and established the right partnerships. Minority and majority firm collaborations can be enhanced by initiatives such as joint ventures and alliances, the creation of joint purchasing councils, the establishment of information and clearing houses, roundtables, and directories (Lichtenstein and Lyons 1996).

Many African American entrepreneurs were ready to face tough challenges head-on to grow their business as noted both in the interviews and in academic research. For instance, a study by Bates (1989) showed that 26 percent of Black Americans who borrowed from banks had larger business and more success than Black Americans who did not borrow from banks.

The interviews along with the research indicated an elevated level of optimism. Kollinger and Minniti (2006) noted that African Americans tend to perceive the environment more optimistically as compared to other ethnic groups.

Concluding Thoughts

This study of African American entrepreneurs is much more than the pursuit of wealth, riches, and the American Dream. These are real-life profiles and viewpoints of African American entrepreneurs quietly traveling on a winding road in America. Almost unrecognized, these entrepreneurs are significant contributors to the economy and sustainability in the African American community. They shape and define America. The entrepreneurs in this study opened their hearts and minds and shared their emotions and thoughts with the world. The authors are forever grateful for their generosity of time and talent.

The research process was, in fact, a long and winding road for the authors. There were numerous discussions concerning the links between race and the entrepreneurs' business-related networking activities, social civic involvement in the community, and outreach efforts. The authors examined the types of business support most beneficial to African Americans during the various stages of business enterprise development.

Understanding the entrepreneurs' development required an understanding of their families, mentors, organizations, and the local or national community contributions to their business growth, their challenges, and mistakes they made during various business-development phases. Insights on what can be done to improve were meticulously gathered (see: http://nxtspark.com/public/blog/).

As professors and consultants to small business owners, the authors worked with various individuals and organizations to gather the viewpoints of over one hundred African American entrepreneurs interviewed for this book. The authors explored their individual experiences, transformations, and knowledge.

The authors focused on the individual entrepreneur. This is their day, their voice, and their story.

After analyzing the interviews and examining the academic literature, the authors found 12 key lessons about African American entrepreneurship.

1. **African American entrepreneurs are constrained by several challenges including the legal system, culture, and financial institutions**—For instance, while legalities such as state, local, and federal mandates for minority participation is helpful, the standardized procedure changes and inconsistent implementation affects the ability of the entrepreneur to plan for their business enterprise meticulously. Cultural disparities with mainstream entrepreneurs along with limited capital access, resources, and workforce can cause adverse effects on the business and life of the African American entrepreneur.

2. **African American entrepreneurs' survival depends on their understanding and acceptance of reality and the need to navigate through the assumptions, biases, stereotypes, and prejudices**—In a day and age where inclusion, diversity, and political correctness is frequently not embraced by the mainstream American, many African American entrepreneurs felt racially profiled in their business endeavors. Several women African American entrepreneurs shared their experiences with race and gender duality, which affected their ability to grow their enterprise and develop professionally.

3. **Social history shapes the African American entrepreneurs. Business, decisions, and actions**—This research endeavor confirmed the importance of entrepreneur's past as an element in business and lifestyle that strongly influences the future. Through family storytelling and shared experiences, African American entrepreneurs are a product of their cultural heritage and history of entrepreneurship that started during slavery. Their history shapes their view of the world, the way they think, and the way they run their enterprise. They are survivors, calculated risk takers capable of overcoming obstacles.

4. **African American entrepreneurs felt economically and socially excluded**—Several entrepreneurs in the study felt they were in some ways unwelcome by the American mainstream businesses. They felt excluded in certain social settings. As a result, many felt compelled to create their own social clubs.

5. **A broader external environment affects African American enterprises**—External factors such as economic climate, government policies, competition, markets, and consumer preferences affect the African American enterprise. There is, therefore, need to be aware of this environment, and include these influencing factors in the business planning process. Being able to pick up situational cues and assess the operating environment accurately is essential.

6. **African American entrepreneurs face limited resource access**—Several interviewed entrepreneurs felt they were constrained by poor capital access, lack of availability of talent skills or ability, and inadequate capabilities about technology among others. Having support in these areas can elevate the performance of African American firms.

7. **Mentors, role models, and community support have positive influences on the African American enterprise**—The interviewed entrepreneurs highlighted the importance of mentors and role models. Several interviewees attributed their success to finding the right mentor. Support from professional organizations and community groups have also contributed to business success.

8. **African American enterprises are going through a transformation process**—Many African American firms are in a state of flux and are constantly adjusting to internal and external changes in their business environment and America. Some of the interviewees attributed

their success to their ability to be flexible and nimble amidst an evolving environment.

9. **Networking is essential to the success of the African American enterprise**—From the gathered interviews, the message was loud and definite. Some majority construction trade entrepreneurs cited networking and positive interactions with the labor as critical to their success's African American construction company owner, also shared the importance of working capital and partnerships with mainstream American construction companies. The African American construction trade owners' ability to work with mainstream businesses and form creative, strategic partnerships and alliances helped in the advancement of several businesses and trade union multimillion dollar construction project as site managers, subcontractors, and vendors.

10. **Community engagement and corporate social responsibility open new doors**—Many of the entrepreneurs chose to be actively involved in the community as workforce development and training advocates and social action projects in their church. They view the community and church as a venue to gather support and to give back to others. Active community engagement helps the entrepreneurs in assessing their operational environment and social capital well, network and access mentors, and other resources.

11. **African American entrepreneurs are practical, flexible, and street-smart survivors**—Many African American entrepreneurs had humble beginnings, and some lived very tough lives. Many have overcome tough obstacles and applied the lessons they learned in life into their own business enterprises. As a result, many African American firms are resourceful and quick to pursue emerging opportunities. These entrepreneurs are not bound to quit so easily. They know what a tough life is, and are prepared to do all they can to grow, prosper, and achieve the American dream. They also embrace others in their community as mentors and resource providers.

12. **African American enterprises have made an impact on the U.S. economy and will grow in number and influence**—African American entrepreneurs are important economic contributors to the U.S. economy. Trends suggest that the number of African American

enterprises will continue to multiply in the future. For example, Georgina Lawton, an entrepreneur and author has leveraged her writing ability to gain a strong influence and following in the African American community (Bustle.com 2017). Cooper-Hudson (2017) cited a National Association of Education Statistics indicating that black women are the most educated segment of the U.S. population. As such, it should not be surprising that black women are the fastest growing group of entrepreneurs in the United States as well (Massie 2016).

In the coming years, their power and influence in the country will increase exponentially.

These lessons and realizations call to light the successes and struggles of African American entrepreneurs and minorities in contemporary America. While their enterprise pathway has typically been long and winded, many have overcome tough obstacles and succeeded.

The authors identified five critical attributes and strategies of successful African American entrepreneurs:

1. **Network extenders**—they cultivated their networks and extended it to create the largest pool of contacts. They used these contacts strategically to gather information, learn, and further their business.
2. **Racial barrier breakers**—they work through racial issues and integrate themselves with the mainstream American firms. They don't let race dampen their entrepreneurial drive and aspirations.
3. **Alliance formers**—they collaborate closely with other businesses, the academe, the government, and the community to advance their business.
4. **Serial reinventors**—they have become an expert in the art of reinventing themselves and their business to succeed. They make frequent business adjustments based on changing circumstances and the often evolving and unpredictable environment.
5. **Active mentors**—they know the value of mentors and have used them extensively in the past. Once successful, they go out of their way to be a mentor to others and share what they know.

The journey the authors took was a quest toward exploring and expand the understanding the African American entrepreneur, the ancestor of unwilling immigrants with a history of survival in the harsh rejecting mainstream American ecosystems. African Americans survived oppression discrimination and limited access to entrepreneurial resources. Many have overcome the toughest challenges. They design the threads of survival threads into a mosaic that generates a sustainable web of resources and support for their enterprise. Their stories, along with their passion for succeeding and strategies for success in a designated zone on a playing field offer valuable lessons that business practitioners, academics, and enthusiasts worldwide can learn from and model.

For the authors, the journey has been partly completed. The research goals were met. However, the interviews conducted were both complete and inadequate. They were complete in a sense that all key questions were asked and answered. They were inadequate because the study further stirred the authors' curiosity. The authors believe that the compiled interviews capture an exciting business perspective of African American entrepreneurs in contemporary America. The interviews are a product of a pioneering exploration and will hopefully encourage similar studies in the future.

As academic explorers, the authors have completed their first trip into the world of African American entrepreneurs. Further exploration beckons.

References

Aeoworks. 2017. *The Tapestry of Black Business Ownership in America: Untapped Opportunities for Business,* available at http://aeoworks.org/images/uploads/fact_sheets/AEO_Black_Owned_Business_Report_02_16_17_FOR_WEB.pdf (accessed July 30, 2017).

Bates, T. 1989. "The Changing Nature of Minority Business: A Comparative Analysis of Asian, Non-Minority and Black-Owned Business." *The Review of Black Political Economy* 18, no. 2, pp. 25–42.

Bates, T. 1994. "Utilization of Minority Employees in Small Business: A Comparison of Non-Minority and Black-Owned Urban Enterprises." *Review of Black Political Economy* 23, no. 1, pp. 113–33.

Bates, T. 1996. "The Financial Capital Needs of Black-Owned Businesses." *The*

Journal of Developmental Entrepreneurship 1, no. 1, pp. 1–15.

Bates, T.M. 1997. *Race, Self-Employment, and Upward Mobility: An Illusive American Dream.* Washington, DC: The Woodrow Wilson Center Press.

Blackdemographics.com 2017. *Black-Owned Businesses,* available at http://blackdemographics.com/economics/black-owned-businesses/ (accessed July 27, 2017).

Brimmer, A., and H. Terrell. 1971. "The Economic Potential of Black Capitalism." *Public Policy* 19, pp. 289–307.

Bustle.com 2017. *Georgina Lawton,* available at https://bustle.com/authors/georgina-lawton-1882 (accessed July 30, 2017).

Captainslog. 2017. *Airline Pilot Challenges,* available at https://captainslog.aero/research/airline-pilot-challenges/ (accessed July 27, 2017).

Cardon, M.S., R.S. Shinnar, M. Eisenman, and E.G. Rogoff. 2008. "Segmenting the Population of Entrepreneurs: A Cluster Study Analysis." *Journal of Developmental Entrepreneurship* 13, no. 3, 293–314. http://webpage.pace.edu/mcardon/index_files/Page774.htm

Cooper-Hudson, M. 2017. *Collaboration is Key to Success for Black Women Entrepreneurs,* available at http://qcitymetro.com/2017/03/07/collaboration-key-success-black-women-entrepreneurs/ (accessed July 30, 2017).

Cummings, S., ed. 1980. *Self-Help in Urban America: Patterns of Minority Business Enterprise.* London: Kennikat Press.

De Freitas, G. 1991. *Inequality at Work: Hispanics in the U.S. Labor Force.* New York, NY: Oxford University Press.

Fairlie, R.W. 1999. "The Absence of the African American Owned Business: An Analysis of the Dynamics of Self-Employment." *Journal of Labor Economics* 17, no. 1, pp. 80–109.

Fairlie, R.W. 2004. "Recent Trends in Ethnic and Racial Business Ownership." *Small Business Economics* 23, no. 3, 203–18. https://ideas.repec.org/p/diw/diwwpp/dp574.html

Fairlie, R.W., and A. Robb. 2007. "Families, Human CapitalHC, and Small BusinessSB: Evidence from the Characteristics of Business Owners Survey." *Industrial and Labor Relations Review* 60, no. 2, pp. 225–45.

Finduslaw. 2017. *Civil Rights ActRA of n1964,* available at https://finduslaw.com/civil-rights-act-1964-cra-title-vii-equal-employment-opportunities-42-us-code-chapter-21 (accessed July 30, 2017).

Fratoe, F.A. 1986. "A Sociological Analysis of Minority Business." *The Review of Black Political Economy* 15, no. 2, 5–29. http://journals.sagepub.com/doi/abs/10.1177/1534484305285459

Harris, J., R. Saltstone, and M. Fraboni. 1999. "An Evaluation of the Job Stress Questionnaire with a Sample of Entrepreneurs." *Journal of Business and Psychology* 13, no. 3, pp. 447–55.

Harwood, E. 1982. "The Sociology of Entrepreneurship." In *Encyclopedia of Entrepreneurship*, eds. C.A. Kent, D.L. Sexton, and K.H. Vesper. Englewood Cliffs, NJ: Prentice Hall.

Hocker, C. 2005. "First to the Starting Line." *Black Enterprise* 35, no. 12, pp. 32–35.

Hout, M., and H. Rosen. 2000. "Self-Employment, Family Background, and Race." *The Journal of Human Resource* 35, no. 4, pp. 670–92.

Kamo, Y. 2000. "Racial and Ethnic Differences in Extended Family Households." *Sociological Perspectives* 43, no. 2, pp. 211–29.

Knight, S. 2017. *Bridging the Gap Through Entrepreneurship. GTE Carolina Small Business Development Fund*, available at https://carolinasmallbusiness. org/2017/02/bridging-the-wealth-gap-through-entrepreneurship/ (accessed July 30, 2017).

Kollinger, P., and M. Minniti. 2006. "Not for Lack of Trying: American Entrepreneurship in Black and White." *Small Business Economics* 27, no. 1, pp. 59–79.

Lee, M.S., E.G. Rogoff, and A.N. Puryear. 1996. "Black Entrepreneurship: It Has the Past, and It Can Have a Future." *The Entrepreneurial Executive* 1, no. 2, pp. 1–9.

Lichtenstein, G., and T.S. Lyons. 1996. *Incubating New Enterprises*. Washington DC: Aspen Institute.

Light, I., and C. Rosenstein. 1995. *Race, Ethnicity, and Entrepreneurship in Urban America*. New York, NY: Aldine Grayton.

Lowrey, Y. 2004. *Dynamics of Minority-Owned Employer Establishments MOEE 1997–2001. Research Paper*. US Small Business Administration, Office of Advocacy.

Lynch, E.W., and M.J. Hanson, eds. 2004. *Developing Cross-Cultural Competence: A Guide for Working with Children and Their Families*. Baltimore, MD: Paul H. Brookes.

Massie, V.M. 2016. *Black Women are the Fastest Growing Group of Entrepreneurs. So where are the investors?* available at https://vox.com/2016/3/14/11208710/ kathryn-finney-diversity-tech (accessed July 30, 2017).

Myers, V. 2017. *Cultural Innovator. A Quote from the Website*, available at http:// vernamyers.com/ (accessed July 26, 2017).

Reddit.com 2017. *Philosophy of Science*, available at https://reddit.com/r/ PhilosophyofScience/comments/587t65/georges_canguilhem_ (accessed July 27, 2017).

Referenceforbusiness.com 2017. *Biography of William Pickard*, available at http:// referenceforbusiness.com/biography/M-R/Pickard-William-F-1941.html (accessed July 27, 2017).

Rhodes, C., and J.S. Butler. 2004. "Understanding Self-Perceptions of Business Performance: An Examination of Black American Entrepreneurs." *Journal of Developmental Entrepreneurship* 9, no. 1, pp. 55–71.

Robb, A.M. 2002. "Entrepreneurial Performance by Women and Minorities: The Case of New Firms." *Journal of Developmental Entrepreneurship* 7, no. 4, pp. 383–97.

Scott, W.L. 1983. "Financial Performance on Minority- Versus Non-Minority-Owned Businesses." *Journal of Small Business Management* 21, no. 1, pp. 42–48.

SBA (Small Business Administration). 2005. *The Small Business Economy for Data Year 2005: A Report to the President.* [www.sba.gov/advo/research/sb_econ2006.pdf]

Sonfield, M.C. 1986. "An Exploratory Analysis of the Largest Black-Owned LBO US Companies." *Journal of Small Business Management* 24, pp. 9–17.

Sonfield, M.C. 2007. "America's Largest Black-Owned Companies: A 30-Year Longitudinal Analysis." *Journal of Developmental Entrepreneurship* 12, no. 3, 323–38.

Tabb, W. 1970. *The Political Economy of the Black Ghetto.* New York, NY: W.W. Norton and Company Inc.

US Census Bureau. 2004. *The Annual Social and Economic Supplement to the Current Population Survey.* Washington, DC: US Department of Commerce.

US Department of Commerce. 2015. *US Minority-Owned Firms Continue to Outpace the Growth of Non-Minority Owned Firms,* available at https://commerce.gov/news/blog/2015/08/us-minority-owned-firms-continue-outpace-growth-nonminority-owned-firms (accessed July 27, 2017).

Walker, E.K. 1999. *The History of Black Business in America.* New York, NY: Macmillan Library Reference USA.

Walstad, W.B., and M.L. Kourilsky. 1998. "Entrepreneurial Attitudes and Knowledge of Black Youth." *Entrepreneurship Theory and Practice* 23, no. 2, pp. 5–18.

Wilson, F., D. Marlino, and J. Kickul. 2004. "Our Entrepreneurial Future: Examining the Diverse Attitudes and Motivations of Teens Across Gender and Ethnic Identity." *Journal of Developmental Entrepreneurship* 9, no. 3, pp. 177–97.

About the Authors

Dr Michelle Ingram Spain is the Director of the Deville School of Business Collaboration Center and Associate Professor at Walsh University. Her publications include a chapter in the book *Contemporary Microenterprise*, and co-authorship of the book *Hispanic Latino Entrepreneurship: Viewpoints of Practitioners*. She designed a Microenterprise Development Model for training the developmentally and physically challenged. She develops minority trade and joint venture partnerships between Ohio business entrepreneurs, Eastern Caribbean, and African entrepreneurs. She has received several awards and recognition such as the SBA Regional Minority Small Business Advocate Award, Small Business Provider Award, Who's Who Cleveland, and Crain's Business Daily 40 Most Influential Women. She is a graduate of Columbia University.

J Mark Munoz is a professor of international business at Millikin University, and a former visiting fellow at Harvard University. He is a recipient of several awards including Best Research Paper Awards, a Literary Award, an International Book Award, and the ACBSP Teaching Excellence Award, among others. He was recognized by the Academy of Global Business Advancement as the 2016 Distinguished Business Dean. Aside from top-tier journal publications, he authored/edited/coedited 17 books including *International Social Entrepreneurship, Contemporary Microenterprises: Concepts and Cases, and Hispanic-Latino Entrepreneurship*. He directs consulting projects for multinational firms and SME's worldwide.

Index

OTHER TITLES IN THE ENTREPRENEURSHIP AND SMALL BUSINESS MANAGEMENT COLLECTION

Scott Shane, Case Western University, Editor

- *Open Innovation Essentials for Small and Medium Enterprises: A Guide to Help Entrepreneurs in Adopting the Open Innovation Paradigm in Their Business* by Luca Escoffier, Adriano La Vopa, Phyllis Speser, and Daniel Satinsky
- *The Technological Entrepreneur's Playbook* by Ian Chaston
- *Licensing Myths & Mastery: Why Most Ideas Don't Work and What to Do About It* by William S. Seidel
- *Arts and Entrepreneurship* by J. Mark Munoz and Julie Shields
- *The Human Being's Guide to Business Growth: A Simple Process for Unleashing the Power of Your People for Growth* by Gregory Scott Chambers

Announcing the Business Expert Press Digital Library

Concise e-books business students need for classroom and research

This book can also be purchased in an e-book collection by your library as

- a one-time purchase,
- that is owned forever,
- allows for simultaneous readers,
- has no restrictions on printing, and
- can be downloaded as PDFs from within the library community.

Our digital library collections are a great solution to beat the rising cost of textbooks. E-books can be loaded into their course management systems or onto students' e-book readers.
The **Business Expert Press** digital libraries are very affordable, with no obligation to buy in future years. For more information, please visit **www.businessexpertpress.com/librarians**. To set up a trial in the United States, please email **sales@businessexpertpress.com**.

Tornado!

Tornado!

Jules Archer

A LUCAS · EVANS BOOK

CRESTWOOD HOUSE
New York
Collier Macmillan Canada
Toronto
Maxwell Macmillan International Publishing Group
New York   Oxford   Singapore   Sydney

For Marsh and Gil and their grandchildren:
Eli, Rhaniel, Daniel, Nina, Norah and Hayden

COVER: Tornado touching down in Union City, Oklahoma, May 24, 1943.
FRONTIS: A powerful tornado hits Cordell, Oklahoma, May 22, 1981.
PAGE 7: Tornado!

PHOTO CREDITS: Cover, Severe Storms Laboratory, Norman, OK; Frontis, Air Weather Service/Public Affairs, NOAA; Page 7, Air Weather Service/Public Affairs, NOAA; Page 11, National Severe Storms Laboratory, Norman, OK; Page 12, Kent & Donna Dannen/Photo Researchers; Pages 14–15, NOAA Photo Library, Rockwell, MD; Page 19, Lowell J. Georgia/Photo Researchers; Page 20, Air Weather Service/Public Affairs, NOAA; Pages 22–23, NOAA Photo Library, Rockwell, MD; Page 25, Air Weather Service/Public Affairs, NOAA; Page 27, Air Weather Service/Public Affairs, NOAA; Page 28, Marine Advisory Program, University of Florida; Page 31, National Severe Storms Laboratory, Norman, OK; Page 33, National Severe Storms Laboratory, Norman, OK; Page 35, National Severe Storms Laboratory, Norman, OK; Page 37, National Severe Storms Laboratory, Norman, OK; Page 38, National Severe Storms Laboratory, Norman, OK; Pages 40–41, Roger Appleton/Photo Researchers; Page 42, C. Clark, National Severe Storms Laboratory, Norman, OK.

BOOK DESIGN: Barbara DuPree Knowles   DIAGRAMS: Andrew Edwards

LIBRARY OF CONGRESS CATALOGING-IN-PUBLICATION DATA
Archer, Jules.
    Tornado! / by Jules Archer.—1st ed.
    p.   cm. — (Nature's disasters)
    SUMMARY: Examines the nature, origins, and dangers of tornadoes and discusses the warning system that detects them and alerts people in their path.
    ISBN 0-89686-594-0
    1. Tornadoes—United States—Juvenile literature.   [1. Tornadoes.]
I. Title.   II. Series.
QC955.5.U6A73   1991   551.55'3—dc20   90-45373

Crestwood House   Collier Macmillan Canada, Inc.
Macmillan Publishing Company   1200 Eglinton Avenue East
866 Third Avenue   Suite 200
New York, NY 10022   Don Mills, Ontario M3C 3N1
                        First Edition
Printed in the United States of America   10 9 8 7 6 5 4 3 2 1

Contents

Tornado!

In April 1986 an Iowa family sought to flee a **tornado** in a pickup truck. The twister roared right over the truck. Their four-year-old girl was sucked up into its **funnel** and disappeared.

Tornadoes blasting over barnyards have stripped chickens of their feathers. Some have snatched blankets and mattresses off beds, leaving sleepers terrified but unharmed. One 1912 tornado plucked a telephone pole out of the ground. Then, as it traveled, it bounced the pole up and down like a pogo stick. In St. Louis in 1896 a tornado drove a two-by-four plank through an iron sheet.

One tornado picked up a locomotive from its track. Then it set the engine down facing the other way on the opposite track. In 1974 a tornado in Xenia, Ohio, sucked up hundreds of trees from an orchard. In West Virginia a 1944 tornado passing over the West Fork River sucked the whole river dry. One woman sought to hide from a tornado in a closet under her back stairway. When she opened the door after the storm, she found that the closet and stairway were all that were left of her house!

These terrifying windstorms can also perform amazing feats of gentleness. One tornado transported a crate of eggs 500 yards without cracking a single shell. Mirrors have been carried for miles and set down unbroken. One jar of pickles traveled 25 miles with a tornado. Then it was lowered unbroken into a ditch.

These exceptions to a tornado's ferocity can be explained. Such objects were lowered through the storm's outer fringes. There, a rising air current let them descend to earth gently.

These stories of tornado freakishness might seem unbelievable. But the National Weather Service has confirmed that they're true.

WHAT IS A TORNADO?

The name "tornado" originally derived from the Latin word *tonare*, to thunder. This developed into the Spanish word *tornear*, to turn or twist. A tornado begins with the formation of a narrow line of thunderstorm clouds. A loud, thunderous roar is produced by the storm. Because a tornado is formed by rotating, or twisting, air, some people call it a twister or cyclone.

A tornado is a powerful column of winds spiraling violently around a center of atmospheric low pressure. In shape it looks like a huge black funnel hanging from a storm cloud. The narrow end sways over the earth. It is like a gigantic anteater sniffing along the ground for ants.

A tornado's winds spiral upward and inward with tremendous speed and power. This creates a vacuum in the funnel that exerts a mighty suction effect on anything the tornado passes over. When the funnel strikes any structure, an explosive effect may cause it to fly apart.

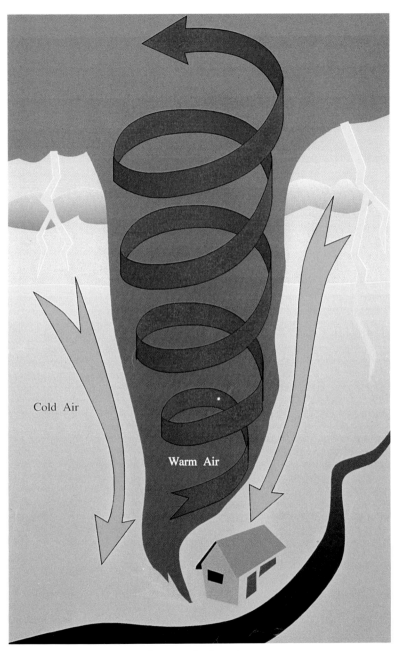

Cold Air

Warm Air

A tornado forming.

The winds inside a tornado may whirl around the center of the storm at speeds up to 400 and 500 miles an hour. The normal speed, however, is usually about 300 miles an hour. That makes these twisters the most dangerous storms known to mankind. In the Northern Hemisphere, most move eastward, rotating counterclockwise. In the Southern Hemisphere, they rotate clockwise. Tornadoes are often heralded by a rain of hailstones. Some hailstones are the size of tennis balls. The largest on record fell on Coffeyville, Kansas, in 1970. It weighed two pounds.

Not every funnel cloud becomes a dangerous tornado. Some never touch down to earth. No one knows why. Those that do may last from a few seconds to a few hours. Some disappear, only to re-form minutes later. The average twister measures 200 to 300 yards across. Some grow large enough to spin off smaller tornadoes, like storm children.

These **satellite tornadoes** can be fierce. Measuring from 50 yards across, they swirl violently around the main funnel. They can do terrible damage. Satellite tornadoes also often branch away. They may take separate paths through a countryside.

A tornado can form suddenly—in a minute sometimes. It can dart across the land with great speed, then abruptly vanish. In a matter of seconds, it can kill dozens of people. Each year tornadoes destroy half a billion dollars' worth of property in the United States.

A Kansas farmer named Will Keller looked directly up into a tornado from his storm cellar near Greensburg on June 22, 1928. He described a circular opening in the center of the funnel, between 50 and 100 feet in diameter. It extended straight up for half a mile. Its walls were spinning clouds. Flashes of lightning let him see into the tornado. He

The tornado that struck Seymour, Texas, on April 10, 1979.

watched small tornadoes constantly form and break away with hissing, snakelike sounds.

Tornadoes are by far nature's most violent and damaging windstorms. No other country has as many as the United States. This is caused by the unique clash of arctic and tropical winds that occurs over the middle states. Each year approximately 850 tornadoes touch down. In 1967 Hurricane Beulah alone spun off 115. It made that year's total a record of 912.

The National Weather Service has been watching, forecasting and reporting tornadoes since 1953. Before then they killed an average of 230 people a year. The deadliest year was 1925, when 689 people died in the twister that struck Missouri, Illinois and Indiana. After the weather service's tornado-warning system went into operation, the death rate dropped sharply. It now averages only 120 people a year. In 1962 only 28 people lost their lives to tornadoes, the best year on record.

Waterspouts—Tornadoes over Water

When a tornado occurs over oceans, lakes or rivers, it is called a **waterspout.** The bottom of the tornado's funnel sucks up water. Waterspouts occur when high layers of cool air blow across a body of water while warm moist air sweeps up from below. They often appear as thin columns above mushroom-shaped water sprays.

Tornado damage in Xenia, Ohio, 1974, left hundreds homeless.

Waterspouts range in size from a few feet to a mile high. They measure from a few feet to hundreds of feet wide. The sounds they make have been described as hissing and sucking noises. They can travel as slow as 2 miles an hour and as fast as 80. Winds within a waterspout can rotate at speeds between 60 and 120 miles an hour. Waterspouts usually last only up to 15 minutes. Few last longer than half an hour.

Like tornadoes, waterspouts often appear in groups. Ships at sea have reported seeing as many as 30 a day.

Waterspouts often draw up and transport astonishing objects. In Montreal they once pelted Canadians with lizards. Waterspouts have rained tadpoles in New York. In France a waterspout even bombarded people with toads. Waterspouts have rained rats on Norwegians and worms on Swedes. One in Providence, Rhode Island, rained fish on the streets. Residents then collected and sold them!

Waterspouts occur most frequently from May to September, over warm ocean water. They are not nearly as dangerous as tornadoes. Nevertheless, they have inflicted serious damage on shipping. One sailing ship, the *Lilian Morris*, encountered a 500-foot-wide waterspout. The spout tore off its masts and sails, and swept a sailor overboard. In 1885 on the North African coast, waterspouts sank five ships in the harbor at Tunis.

What Conditions Breed Tornadoes?

The thunderclouds that produce tornadoes tend to develop when different temperatures and humidity meet. This often occurs in the United States when warm, wet winds from the Gulf of Mexico blow north in spring and early summer. They meet colder, dry Canadian winds blowing south over

Giant waterspouts.

the Rocky Mountains at about 50 miles an hour. These winds are also joined by an eastward-moving, 300-mile river of cold air, called the jet stream. It travels up to 8 miles overhead at 150 miles an hour or faster.

The boundary where the Gulf and Canadian winds meet is called a **dry line.** The high, dry air coming off the Rockies piles on top of the low, moist Gulf air at a height of over 10,000 feet. The warm winds from the south try to rise. The cold northern air blocks them. This clash of winds causes some trapped warm air to whirl horizontally between the two air masses. Meanwhile, the sun keeps making the earth below hotter. The rising warm winds finally become strong enough to punch through the cold air layer.

When this happens, the higher cold air begins to sink. That sends the rising warm winds spinning upward like a corkscrew. They whirl faster and faster in a tall column. When this updraft is strong, it can soar to heights of 10 miles or more. It spins at speeds of up to 100 miles an hour. The swirling winds produce immense storm clouds close to 70,000 feet high. They often spread 10 miles wide.

The storm system may be strong enough to stay intact for several hours. Then its thunderclouds are called **supercells**. They can drop an inch of rain in just ten minutes. They can also blanket the ground with hail the size of baseballs. Supercells can grow into great clusters. They sometimes form a squall line nearly 100 miles long. These can develop one or more **mesocyclones.**

(OPPOSITE PAGE) Warm and cold air masses clash above the midwestern U.S., producing the violent winds that have earned the region the nickname "Tornado Alley."

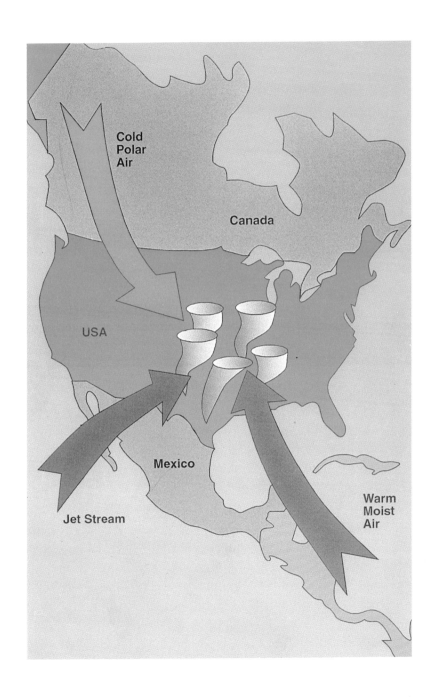

The Mesocyclone—Mother of Tornadoes

The mesocyclone (mess-o-sy-klon) is a column of wind that narrows and spins more and more fiercely. It stretches both upward and downward through the supercells. A wall cloud swirls with it and makes it visible. It has the appearance of a huge, boiling black cloud bulging down from the supercells. It can measure from half a mile to six miles wide.

A mesocyclone may not always produce a tornado. Some 1,700 mesocyclones a year hit various parts of the United States. Only about half produce tornadoes. If the mesocyclone runs out of moist, warm surface air, it simply dies out. It may not run out of that fuel, however. Then the ominously rotating black cloud continues to stretch toward the ground.

The entire wall cloud of the mesocyclone may be transformed into a giant tornado. Or one may simply drop from it. Some observers report that either is most likely to happen when mesocyclone clouds appear yellow or green. It may also happen when the air is muggy and still—after the rain and hail have stopped.

Tornadoes almost always appear on the right rear side of thunderclouds. They take place close to where a stream of cool air from the downdraft spins into the main updraft of warm air.

The mesocyclone may drop not just one, but a whole family of tornadoes. These spin around the mother funnel like small gears around a giant wheel. One storm on February 19, 1884, brought 60 tornadoes in a single day.

(OPPOSITE PAGE) A farmhouse in Blue Springs, Nebraska, destroyed by a tornado in 1973.

18

How Powerful? How Long?

Tornadoes rated F-0 and F-1 can damage chimneys and thrust mobile homes off their foundations. They can push cars off roads. F-2 and F-3 tornado winds can tear roofs off houses. They can lift and toss heavy cars. F-4 and F-5 tornadoes can pluck up and carry buildings a distance. They can toss steel beams and crunch cars.

F-4 and F-5 tornadoes appear less frequently than the others. But such monster twisters do most of the killing. They are responsible for two-thirds of the 120 or so tornado deaths in the United States each year. Tornadoes kill twice as many people as hurricanes.

They may last from a few seconds to over nine hours.

Aircraft damaged by a tornado at an air force base in Oklahoma.

Tornado Lightning and Sound Effects

During one Oklahoma tornado, as many as 24,000 lightning flashes were recorded. Some scientists think that these discharges of electricity may be the real driving force behind tornadoes.

Lightning between clouds seems most intense when the mesocyclone reaches its peak. Mesocyclone lightning is described as more brilliant, bluer and more "vicious" than ordinary lightning.

One man described the sound of a tornado as a "sustained, hollow roaring, like a distant freight train." Some have reported hearing a peculiar hissing, whistling noise. Other descriptions have likened a tornado's sound to the roar of hundreds of locomotives, thousands of cannons or "the buzzing of millions of bees."

One man reported feeling the sound vibrate the air against his eardrums and throb against his face.

How Do Tornadoes Behave?

Scientists can never be sure how a tornado will behave. Its funnel may touch the ground, or may never reach the ground at all. Then again, it may touch down, bounce back up and vanish. Or the funnel may touch down once, rise up and travel a long distance, and then suddenly touch down again. A tornado may move in circles or spin in the same spot for 20 minutes. Or it may cut a zigzag path for miles.

When a tornado touches the earth, its narrow neck may measure from 50 yards to as wide as a mile. It generally moves along at about 40 miles an hour. It cuts a path 10 to 40 miles long. But some tornadoes have roared along a

Tornado lightning.

murderous path over 2 miles wide and almost 300 miles long.

The shape of a tornado may vary. It may look like a long, thin rope or a fat, upside-down bell. Its length, from the base of the funnel to the tip of its "elephant trunk," can measure between 800 and 2,000 feet. Faster upper winds usually blow the top of the funnel cloud more swiftly than the lower end. That seems to drag behind. Earth friction adds to the drag effect.

Tornadoes behave like insane giants displaying enormous strength. One once lifted a 70-ton railroad coach off its tracks and flung it into a ditch 80 feet away. In Canada a dishwasher was blown from the city of Edmonton into a farmer's field 20 miles away. One tornado sucked an auto 200 feet up in the air and dropped it in a field. Its driver was killed. Another destroyed a house, carrying its refrigerator a quarter of a mile. It landed on the roof of a bank.

WHERE TORNADOES STRIKE

Tornadoes occur all over the world, but mostly in the United States. The only state that has escaped tornadoes is Alaska. One third of all U.S. tornadoes strike Oklahoma, Texas and Kansas. These three states are part of a dozen Great Plains states known as Tornado Alley. The city that has suffered the greatest number of tornadoes is Oklahoma City.

The earliest American record of a tornado comes from a colonist in 1643. He described one that hit a Massachusetts meeting house and killed an Indian. In 1761 a fierce tornado struck Charleston, South Carolina. It sank five warships in the harbor and smashed houses and trees onshore.

Tornadoes take many forms.

Early pioneers traveling west across the Great Plains reported seeing tornadoes suck up buffalo, carry them overland, then spew them out.

In England, as early as 1091, a tornado was reported to have destroyed 600 houses. In 1638 another twister in England struck a church during a service. It wrecked the roof and tower, and killed 60 people. The vicar blamed "the devil."

But no tornadoes outside the United States have caused death and destruction on the scale of the powerful twisters.

TORNADO VICTIMS
DESCRIBE THE EXPERIENCE

A tornado struck McKinney, Texas, in June 1951. It trapped retired army captain Roy S. Hall and his family inside the funnel. The bottom of the funnel was about 20 feet above the ground.

Hall reported a tremendous jolt. The floor slid under his feet, almost throwing him. His hat was yanked off his head. All around him, objects flashed upward. He sensed that the roof of the house was gone. The side of a room crashed in as if driven by a gigantic sledgehammer. He was blown 10 feet away.

He found himself looking up into the interior of a great tornado funnel. It seemed hollow to him, with 10-foot-thick cloud walls. The funnel was rotating at great speed. It extended upward for over a thousand feet. It swayed and bent toward the southeast.

Although their house was destroyed, Hall and his family miraculously survived. But the tornado roared through

A typical funnel-shaped tornado.

McKinney. More than 100 people were killed and injured. It did over $5 million worth of property damage.

In Ponca City, Oklahoma, a tornado lifted a house while a couple was eating supper inside. The house exploded around them. Then the tornado winds settled the floor back to the ground. The dumbstruck couple was unharmed.

A tornado snapped trees and lifted this house off its foundation.

During another tornado, one woman sought to escape and jumped into her bathtub. She pulled a mattress over herself. Her house was blown away. All that survived were the bathtub, the mattress and the woman.

One day Southern Railroad engineer E. F. Shine found his train racing headlong into an Ohio tornado. He decided to risk plunging through the twisting funnel at top speed. He opened the throttle all the way. Then he crouched down in the cab. The day turned black. The air was filled with a terrible roar.

Howling tornado winds peeled off the steel roof of the cab. Shine felt a powerful suction pulling him up. He clung to his seat with all his strength. Then the train shot through the tornado funnel into daylight. Shine and the train were saved.

School Children in Tornadoes

In 1989 a 100-mile-an-hour tornado struck the East Coldenham, New York, elementary school. More than 120 children were eating lunch in the two-story cafeteria. The fierce blast struck the yellow brick-and-glass building. A huge section of one wall crashed down onto the children. Those standing to watch were tossed about like rag dolls.

"I heard a whistling sound," said Mike Miller, age seven. "Tables were flying. Bricks were flying. There was breaking glass. People were crying." Teachers tore at the rubble, trying to reach the fallen children. In the end, 7 children died and 18 were hospitalized. The firemen who rescued them wept in pity.

Some children have been luckier. Several students in Ohio were rehearsing a play when a tornado struck their high school. They fled the auditorium when the roof and walls began caving in. Seconds later two school buses were blown into the building. They crashed on the stage where the students had been rehearsing.

One Midwest twister that demolished a schoolhouse carried frightened children 150 yards. Then it set them down without killing or seriously injuring any of them.

The best film record we have of a tornado was made by a teenager on April 3, 1974. Bruce Boyd, 16, had not yet used his new movie camera when a tornado struck his hometown, Xenia, Ohio. He aimed the camera at the approaching twister, which was swaying in the sky ahead. Transfixed, he kept the camera whirring as the tornado smashed houses and sucked up trees. At the last minute, he dived for cover with the camera, escaping harm. Six months later, NBC-TV broadcast Bruce's dramatic record of the killer storm.

THE TORNADO WARNING SYSTEM

In 1870 the U.S. government wanted to give citizens of Tornado Alley some indication of when and where tornadoes would hit. The job was given to the U.S. Army Signal Corps.

The corps decided to issue only warnings or "probabilities" of "severe local storms." The corps worried that a specific forecast of a tornado striking a town or area would cause panic.

When the National Weather Service took over the job, that policy of caution continued. In 1896 its forecasters were sure that tornadoes were about to strike heavily populated Saint Louis. But they predicted only "local thunderstorms." Tornadoes killed 100 unprepared residents of the city that day. Nearly 100 more died in East Saint Louis.

A public uproar rocked the weather service. It then felt compelled to begin making specific predictions of tornadoes.

During World War II, many war-production plants and army air bases were built in the Midwest. Tornadoes did severe damage to them. So the weather service began working with the army to build a network of tornado watchers. These volunteers phoned a weather service or airfield station the moment funnel clouds were spotted. Officials then radioed or phoned tornado warnings to towns, factories and airfields in the paths of danger.

In 1973 the weather service began using scientific instruments to chase and chart tornadoes across the Great Plains. The studies that resulted enabled the service to make better predictions of tornado strength, size and behavior. And where and when to expect them.

Scientists at work at the National Severe Storms Forecast Center.

A tornado chase team intercepts a 1984 twister.

We have learned a great deal more about tornadoes in recent years. This has resulted from scientific studies by the National Severe Storms Laboratory (NSSL) in Norman, Oklahoma, the heart of Tornado Alley. Scientists there cooperate with researchers from the University of Oklahoma and other universities.

The Tornado Chasers

NSSL scientists send out teams to locate and intercept tornadoes without getting trapped by them. The teams remain in touch with their bases by radio and mobile phone. Their roving vans are equipped with computer-controlled electronic equipment. Video cameras operate by remote control from the van roofs.

The chase teams used to drop a 400-pound unit called a **TOTO** (Totable Tornado Observatory) in the path of a tornado. This measured its wind speed, temperature, direction and atmospheric pressure. The TOTO, however, was usually blown over as soon as a tornado gale reached 150 miles an hour. Since 1987 it has been replaced by a portable Doppler radar unit with a range of 3 to 5 miles.

This device can identify a mesocyclone some two to four hours before it drops or develops into a tornado. It can also detect whether tornado winds are moving toward or away from it—and how fast.

The tornado chasers often find themselves in tight spots. They try to get close enough to a tornado to observe the inside of its funnel. However, the twister may move faster than expected. Or it may suddenly change direction and bear down on them. The chasers' lives depend on gunning their motors to escape quickly.

TOTO:
a measuring device
dropped in the path
of a tornado.

Every April and May, NSSL researchers spend hundreds of hours racing over western Oklahoma roads. They try to catch fast-moving mesocyclones in the very act of spinning out tornadoes.

Tornado Watches and Warnings

In 1969 the Environmental Science Services Administration (**ESSA**) set up a program called **SKYWARN.** This expanded the network of volunteer tornado spotters. More people became involved in spreading warnings and getting people quickly to safety.

A special National Severe Storms Forecast Center (SELS) operates from Kansas City, Missouri. It keeps track of mesocyclones that may spew out tornadoes. When weather conditions indicate the possibility of a tornado, SELS issues a **tornado watch.**

This indicates that tornadoes may occur during the next several hours in a specific area. The size of the area is about 100 miles wide and 250 miles long. It advises people there to be ready to take shelter at once if a tornado is actually sighted. These alerts are issued to local weather stations, TV and radio stations, and the tornado-spotter network, which includes ham radio operators.

It is up to local weather stations to issue **tornado warnings** when twisters have actually been sighted or detected by radar. Tornadoes reveal themselves on weather station radar as the revolving ball of a "6" figure dangling from a mesocyclone image. Tornado warnings then are sent out swiftly over TV and radio. They report areas in danger, times of detection and expected strikes.

Deciding when to issue a tornado watch is a delicate job for SELS. Frederick P. Ostby, director of the forecasting center in Kansas City, explains that the United States gets about 100,000 thunderstorms a year. Only 1 percent, or 1,000, produce tornadoes. Only 2 percent of the tornadoes cause 70 percent of the deaths. The center tries to determine whether those 20 or so killer tornadoes will appear. Its goal is to put a watch out two to six hours ahead of time.

There is a danger in putting out too many tornado watches that prove to be false alarms: People will stop paying attention to them. But most people in Tornado Alley have learned to take seriously the watches that are put out. In the eastern United States, however, the situation is differ-

A Doppler radar unit in Norman, Oklahoma.

ent. There, people don't often see tornadoes. So they ignore the watches—until a tornado *does* strike their area.

Many communities in Tornado Alley have set up alarm systems. These go into action when the local weather station issues a tornado warning. The public may be alerted by radio and TV announcements, fire sirens or civil defense sirens. Farmers in threatened rural areas may be warned by phone.

The importance of tornado warnings was demonstrated in Leedey, Oklahoma, in May 1947. A telephone official

copy 1 **35**

there sighted a tornado funnel approaching in the distance. He at once sounded the fire alarm and also spread the warning through a public address system. When the twister struck Leedey, two-thirds of the town was destroyed. But there were only six casualties. Almost all of Leedey's citizens had fled into basements or storm cellars before the killer tornado tore through.

Warnings are extremely valuable even when they give people only a few minutes' time to hide or get out of the way. Those few minutes can mean the difference between life and death.

PREVENTING TORNADO DAMAGE

Perhaps the best protection against tornadoes is a safe, well-built house. It should be strong enough to defy a twister. Engineers and architects recommend walls of reinforced concrete. They should be well anchored to the foundation. A good solid roof can be secured with strap anchors over the rafters.

Many who live in Tornado Alley without such strong houses have built storm cellars. A storm cellar should be separate from the house. It should be located near the southwest corner of the house, not too close to house walls. Its doors should open inward in case storm debris blocks the exit. The cellar should have good drainage to prevent flooding.

People in tornado country used to be advised to open house windows before leaving for shelter. As in hurricanes, this precaution was presumed to keep a house from exploding. But new studies now indicate that it is best to keep all windows closed against tornadoes.

Inside the Doppler dome—a huge radar antenna.

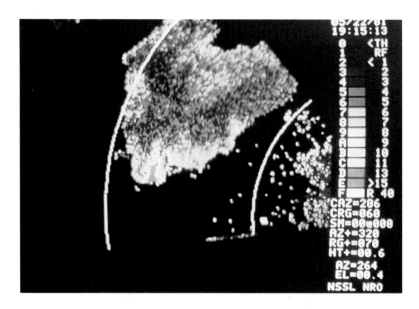

How a tornado appears on the radar screen of a Binger Doppler.

Hiding from Tornadoes

A tornado watch should make you extremely alert. This is especially important if the weather is uncomfortably warm, humid and oppressive, with dark thunderclouds in the western and northern sky. Be prepared for the watch to become a tornado warning. That happens if dark cloud masses begin bulging downward like huge balloons.

Keep a battery-powered radio tuned to local stations. If you spot a funnel cloud, you may have no more than five minutes to find shelter. If you actually hear the roar of a tornado, you will have only seconds.

When a tornado warning is issued, or tornado sirens sound, hurry to the nearest storm cellar or shelter. It should contain blankets, bottled water, transistor radios and first-aid supplies.

If no storm cellar or town shelter is available, crouch in the southwest corner of your basement. If there is no basement, flatten out on the floor under heavy furniture or a bed. As mentioned, one person successfully protected herself in a bathtub under a mattress! Others have survived under stairwells or in closets.

Stay away from windows, which can be pierced by flying debris. For further protection, surround yourself with a thick blanket. Put as many walls as possible between you and the outside.

If a tornado catches you in school, keep away from windows. Move to a section of the building with inside walls. A hallway, basement or stairwell is fine.

If you are outdoors in a car, stop and seek shelter in a building. Or head for a ditch or ravine. Lie facedown and cover your head. Don't be caught standing. You could be killed by broken glass, pipes or lumber flying around in the funnel.

Car drivers may risk trying to outrace a 25-mile-an-hour tornado. But a sudden change in the twister's direction can trap the car and its occupants. A rolling, pitching, twisting auto is a death trap.

Keep a battery-operated radio tuned for the latest news and instructions. Don't leave your shelter or position until you hear that the tornado has ended—or an ALL CLEAR siren sounds.

TOMORROW'S TORNADO WARNING SYSTEMS

Continual research by the National Severe Storms Forecast Center is helping meteorologists explore many tornado phenomena that are still puzzling. They want to know what actually triggers a tornado. Is lightning a factor? They hope

Remains of a gas station in Colorado Springs, Colorado.

41

to find out why most tornadoes are relatively weak while a few develop into terrifying blockblusters. Also, why do some have longer damage paths than others? Does a funnel's wind speed change during its sweep? Are those winds more powerful in mile-wide tornadoes than in smaller ones?

The nation's warning system is likely to improve during the 1990s. The government plans to replace the weather service's ordinary radar with computerized Dopplers. These units are called Next-Generation Weather Radar. This system will track and analyze mesocyclones better than ordinary radar can. Once a Doppler detects a mesocyclone, 20 minutes or more may pass before a tornado touches down. That should give local forecasters a good time lead to warn nearby communities to seek shelter.

A second network of radar called Profilers is also expected to be in place by 1995. The Profilers will measure winds in the upper atmosphere as high up as 20 miles. They will

The work of a tornado in Newkirk, Oklahoma, April 18, 1978.

help predict possible mesocyclones. The Profilers will be complemented by radiosonde reports from weather balloons. These give wind direction and speed at different altitudes.

There were angry complaints when a tornado struck Illinois on Tuesday, August 28, 1990. The storm took 25 lives, injured over 100 people and caused great property damage. Only a severe thunderstorm warning was in place when the tornado struck. The tornado warning was not issued until 21 minutes later. Dr. Frederick P. Ostby, director of the National Severe Storms Forecast Center, explained why this happened. The tornado had not been detected earlier, he said, because a radar device had been put out of action by lightning prior to the storm. He also noted that only about half of all tornadoes can be detected in time to issue a tornado watch. The tornado warning system is still an imperfect science. But it is steadily being improved.

The government hopes to increase advance warning times of mesocyclones and tornadoes. It plans to place hundreds of automated weather evaluators around remote areas of the West.

Some research is being directed at trying to weaken the powerful energy potential of mesocyclones. One technique being studied is seeding the mesocyclones with dry ice to prevent tornadoes from forming. The hope is to induce heavy rainfall, thus robbing the mesocyclones of their strength. So far such experiments have failed.

Still, if all Americans learn to respect the erratic nature of tornadoes and seek shelter quickly when warnings are issued, fewer people will fall victim to these whirling killers from the sky.

Some Famous

1840   Natchez, Mississippi: Newspaper headline: HORRIBLE
       STORM!! NATCHEZ IN RUINS!!! Over 370 dead.

1896   St. Louis, Missouri: A tornado doing $13 million in prop-
       erty damage kills 306 people.

1924   Lake Erie cities: Tornadoes raging for 40 minutes kill 99.
       People, horses, cars, trees and debris are hurled through
       the streets.

1925   The Tri-State Tornado kills 689 and injures over 3,000 in
       Missouri, Illinois and Indiana. It's the most destructive
       twister known in history. Whole towns are demolished.

1936   Mississippi and Georgia: Two days of powerful tornadoes
       leave 658 people dead.

1965   The Palm Sunday Tornadoes rampage for nine hours
       through six states from Iowa to Ohio. They cost the area
       271 dead, 5,000 injured and $300 million in property
       damage.

1967   Texas: Hurricane Beulah spins off over 155 tornadoes.
       These whirl off to add to the hurricane damage.

44

Tornadoes

1974   Five states from Alabama to Ohio suffer a superoutbreak of 148 tornadoes. Dead: 350. Property destroyed: over $1 *billion* worth. A 47-car freight train is picked up and flung onto the main street.

1979   Wichita Falls, Texas: A ten-mile-high tornado carves an eight-mile path of death and destruction. Cars are bent around telephone poles. Death toll: 60.

1985   Ohio Valley and Canada. A series of 41 tornadoes leaves 90 dead, over 1,000 injured. Giant 40-ton gas storage tanks are lifted, crushed and tossed across a road.

1990   Huntsville, Alabama: A tornado devastates a ten-mile-long, quarter-mile-wide path. A woman and her three sons crouch in their bathroom. Seconds later that room is the only one left standing in the house.

1990   Seven Midwest states from Wisconsin to Kansas suffer a deadly barrage of tornadoes that leave 24 cities severely damaged. In one four-hour period, 50 tornadoes touch down. Death toll: 13.

Glossary

dry line The boundary where winds from the Gulf of Mexico and Canada meet and clash.

ESSA Environmental Science Service Administration, replaced by NOAA (National Oceanic and Atmospheric Administration) in 1970.

funnel The spinning cloud that reaches down to earth from the storm.

mesocyclone The column of storm winds stretching upward and downward through the storm clouds, and from which the tornado funnels drop.

satellite tornadoes Smaller tornadoes that spin off from major tornadoes and may go their own way.

SKYWARN ESSA's (later NOAA) network of volunteer tornado spotters.

supercells The storm clouds that give birth to mesocyclones and their tornadoes.

tornado A powerful column of winds spiraling violently around a center of atmospheric low pressure.

tornado warning The next stage of a weather alert after a tornado watch. It advises people in an area that one or more tornadoes are likely to occur.

tornado watch The first weather alert advising people that tornadoes may strike.

TOTO A device dropped in the path of a tornado to measure its strength, speed and direction.

waterspout A moving column of water drawn up by a whirlwind at sea and meeting a descending, funnel-shaped cloud.

For Further Reading

Alth, Max, and Charlotte Alth. *Disastrous Hurricanes and Tornadoes.* New York: Franklin Watts, 1981.
Bixby, William. *Skywatchers.* New York: David McKay Company, 1962.
Buehr, Walter. *Storm Warning: The Story of Hurricanes & Tornadoes.* New York: William Morrow & Co., Inc., 1972.
Laffoon, Polk. *Tornado.* New York: Harper & Row, 1975.
Smith, Howard E., Jr. *Killer Weather.* New York: Dodd, Mead & Company, 1982.
Tufty, Barbara. *1001 Questions Answered about Storms.* New York: Dodd, Mead & Company, 1970.
Winchester, James H. *Hurricanes, Storms, Tornadoes.* New York: G. P. Putnam's Sons, 1968.

INDEX